From The

HEART

of

CHILDHOOD

Reclaiming Presence for Connection

J U L I E   L A M

From The Heart of Childhood:

Reclaiming Presence for Connection
Copyright © 2025 by Julie Lam

Hardcover ISBN: 978-1-967575-09-1
Paperback ISBN: 978-1-967575-08-4
eBook ISBN: 978-1-967575-10-7
Printed in the USA.

Joan of Arc Publishing
Meridian, ID 83646
www.joapublishing.com

Enjoy Exclusive Bonuses!

Thank you for reading *From the Heart of Childhood.*
As a special thank you, I've created exclusive
bonuses just for you.

How to Access Your Book Bonuses

Simply scan the QR code below with your phone
to unlock your special resources:

The healing you seek lives within childhood's sacred realm.

In these transformative times, this book offers a profound invitation to reconnect with your essence while deepening your capacity to truly see others.

Whether healing your own inner child or nurturing others as a parent, teacher, or companion, this revolutionary approach to presence becomes the foundation of all loving relationships.

Through exploring three developmental phases—Truth in the Body (age 0–7), Beauty in the Soul (age 7–14), and Goodness in the Spirit (age 14–21)—discover how childhood's sacred doorways stand open, waiting for you to step across the threshold into healing and wholeness.

In a world marked by disconnection, this gentle journey guides you to:

- Reconnect with your body's innate wisdom, where trust and security first formed;

- Reawaken your heart's capacity for wonder, imagination, and authentic connection;

- Reclaim your voice and purpose through understanding your conscious mind's development.

Through practices of sacred listening and compassionate witnessing, discover how the wounds of disconnection become gateways to profound healing.

This is not just a book but a sanctuary where forgotten parts of yourself are welcomed home and where you learn to create that same sanctuary for others. It is a calling to reclaim the stillness of presence and the warmth of true connection—creating the current that heals, transforms, and reminds us of the wholeness we've always been.

TABLE OF
CONTENTS

DEDICATION

To My Family,

For my husband, Man, I felt I knew you before I met you! I am so grateful for all we have learnt (and still are) about how to love and what the practice of faithfulness means: to see the truth of who we are, for each other, through all of our seasons.

For our children: Laura, Edward, Jeremy, and Harry, who have guided me to the power of presence and the courage of heartfelt connection—teaching me the art of real imperfect parenting. You each reveal the beauty of your individual spirit, and show me the healing and joy found in the present moment. You are the heart of this book, my greatest teachers.

For my grandchildren, Sebastian and Otto, who have strengthened my voice as a guardian of childhood's wonder. Through your eyes, you keep the magic of raindrops alive in me and show me the art of holding space for the present moment.

For my own grandmothers whose gift of time and attention showed me that love is an active choice—a daily practice. Their wise words continue to echo through my life, to be passed on through the generations.

For my dearest parents, who planted the seeds of who I would become: my mother, whose determination and consistency formed the foundation of my journey, and my father, whose open, tender heart taught me the quiet power of soft love.

For Sally, my sister and first companion in childhood's journey, whose life has intertwined with mine through shared memories that shaped us differently yet bound us eternally—your generosity, humour, and playful spirit illuminate what beauty in the heart truly means.

Through each of you, I have felt love's ability to heal, transform, and awaken—the living truth that weaves throughout this book.

"Receive the children in reverence;

Educate them in love,

Let them go forth in freedom."

~Rudolf Steiner
(quoted in *Highgate House School Parent Handbook*, 2003)

PROLOGUE

High on The Peak over the city of Hong Kong there is a beautiful oasis that is closely connected to my heart. It is frequently shrouded in mist and clouds throughout the long months of the humid season, and there are great and wonderful stories that have unfolded within the magical spaces of the rooms and the garden. There is the sound of children at play, which seems to echo long after they have all returned home at the end of the day.

I have lived in this international city for forty years. After my marriage I was able to fully experience life within the local community, and I immersed myself with interest in the rich tapestry of cultures from all over the world. Throughout these decades, I've moved through great challenges and received profound gifts brought by Hong Kong's transient nature, all while nurturing the continuation of this unique and long-standing preschool.

This school is a sanctuary; it is a place for children, a homelike place. It is also a place for parents, teachers, families, and the ones who organise, clean, plan, —a place for a whole community.

It is a school that I birthed into existence and cared for through the years. I've rejoiced with it, sometimes resented it, and painfully grieved over it during difficult times. The empty, forlorn rooms during enforced closures—through the SARS virus outbreak, the city's political protests, and the worldwide Covid crisis—left lasting impressions. It all began in 1992 with the support of two other mothers. Now it is supported by my husband, my daughter, and myself.

As I write, the school still stands, yet for several recent years, it has faced an uncertain future. Times are changing, and as we move with the changes and uncertainty, a new sense of direction has appeared. I've been discovering the quiet space of wisdom that lives within each of us—a place we can all access. When I take a moment to step back from all the mental chatter and stories I tell myself, I find answers and peace that were there all along. This isn't some special gift—it's something we all have, like a natural wellspring that's always flowing beneath the surface of our busy lives. Finding this connection has been my greatest strength during uncertain times, and I believe it can be yours too. My deepest wish now is to help others tap into this same inner knowing, to remember their own power that's been there from the beginning.

I feel fulfilled and thankful for the greatest gifts brought by the living essence of the school, the life lessons for me, and for us all—a whole community of young and old—who have, over the years, been part of the shared journey. I am in deep gratitude to all the children who have gifted their families, teachers, and all the members of our team with their wonder and wisdom. Between school and the home we have worked, connecting and building bridges between each other as colleagues, professionals, parents, and friends.

Highgate House School, a place to breathe, has shaped the expression of who I am today. And its foundations are rooted in a dedication to honour the unique expression of each child who has found their way through the doors to absorb the unique beauty of the classrooms, the magic of the play, the joys of the garden, the friendships, and most importantly the gentle caregiving. It has guided my learning, touched me deeply, and expanded my heart.

In this magical preschool, as in our lives, we have felt both supportive connections *and* the pain of disconnection, often stemming from deep misunderstandings and narrow veiled perceptions, and yet we've had such great learning as so many diverse cultures have come together to teach us to open up, through the beauty of our shared projects; and so many meetings over the years as we have searched for ways to let everyone be heard, all whilst moving through the joys and challenges of living and working together.

We have experienced an inability to listen to each other, fear of sharing our deepest feelings, and frustrating broken communications— that we often blamed on cultural differences. Looking deeper, these conflicts stemmed from our fixed beliefs and our own childhood wounds, frequently causing us to fall into self-defense created from fears we couldn't even name.

We have connected most powerfully when we have been willing to listen more deeply, finding a voice for each person to bring to our meetings. Together, we've tried to lead as a community while balancing individual needs with the whole for the greater good.

We have raised ourselves up when we have been able to bring ourselves to each other fully present. And then we have learned new ways of seeing.

It has been continual learning. Typhoons of emotions come and go. People come and go. And we crack open our hearts, moving through each challenge, touched in the heart by the children who help us see the true beauty of our lives unfolding exactly as they are meant to.

It has been the children who have been our greatest teachers, we have eventually come to see. They are the lighters of wisdom, the call to unite us, calling us back to the present moment with the invitation to remember who we are and what we came here to do.

"Childhood lies at the heart of who we are and who we will become."

~ Fred Rogers

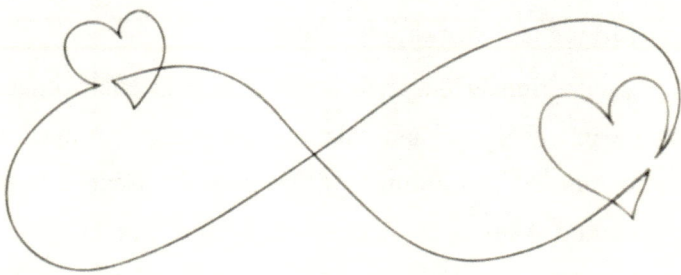

It is time to reclaim the transformative power of deep, heart-centred connection. In the sacred quiet of your inner being lies an unchanging presence—the essence of your true being that never leaves you. This presence, so often forgotten in our busy world, is your first home, your essential nature, the place of healing and awakening to what is.

This book offers a pathway back through the heart of childhood, to return to your centre, and to bring the authentic connection that heals divisions and reveals beauty in a shared love of truth.

In these unsettling times, we need the profound connections that unite us. Now, more than ever before, we need to focus on nurturing and healing our capacity for presence and connection: a connection to the sacred space within where our human nature meets our spiritual origin; a connection between our hearts to bring kindness and understanding for each other; and a connection to our bond with the earth that sustains us.

Our childhood journeys, with their inevitable wounds and disconnections, are not meaningless suffering but profound invitations to remember what matters most: they are the call back, and our beautiful reminder, of how to return to presence; and from that still place, to remember we are born to connect to each other from the wholeness that we are.

Every interaction in our lives is a lesson in love; every relationship is a sacred exchange. Each encounter is an invitation to see our own being more clearly, to step through a gateway to more love in our lives and to choose to share that with others.

BEYOND SURFACE AUTHENTICITY

What do we mean by "authentic connection"?

It is common today to hear people use the phrase "claiming my authentic self," and the word "authenticity" can start to feel cliché, depending on the meaning we make of it.

Many associate being authentic with individual rights, asserting power, believing it is a responsibility to voice our disagreement at any time or place, often at the expense of giving time to understand others. Ironically, we use it like a badge, creating identities that get us approval, and yet we are still dissatisfied as we feel we are not truly seen and accepted for who we really are.

Return to the natural presence always within you. Rest in open awareness. Rediscover deep compassion for others and allow it to return to fill you, revealing the beautiful truth that there is no separation between us.

This may sound idealistic, unachievable, and for some people even unbelievable. Even now I hear a critical voice in my mind still trying to correct me to "come down from the clouds, those misty clouds high up," and "get real." Yes, I hear you, and I answer, "I promise to be real. This is reality, perhaps the most real part of our experience. This isn't about escaping life; it's about fully showing up for it."

And I also promise you, this doorway to presence is always open. It only requires your open curiosity and your wish to come back to the quiet awareness of your being.

From our still centre we can connect to the flow of attention, not the distracted half-awareness we have grown accustomed to but the full, loving recognition of our own experience and that of another soul's being.

The pathway will help you release tightness in your heart, tension in your limbs, and darkness in your mind. You don't need to explore alone, for I am here, and I will go with you.

This book is a guide along a path you may find has a different feel.

It is not a factual instruction manual to tell you how to heal, how to parent, or how to teach.

It is an image of the natural emerging of your whole being, of phases of childhood, each one revealing a new way of seeing as we follow the unfolding wonder of body, heart, and mind to find greater insights into the nature of who we are.

It is a rediscovery of attention and presence, to directly see that the gifts for ourselves and our children are found within each arc of our developmental journey.

We will discover together the jewels hidden within each of us. In every phase we can see how to bring what is needed, healing our sense of lack to find the ease, the peace, and the happiness that frees us all.

In our adulthood, we know deep down that we are not just physical bodies with a mind made for thoughts. The human being is made up of layers—each aspect of ourselves building upon the other—that work in harmony, each part needed.

From birth, on our human journey, we need time to unfold each layer, honouring the unique pace and process.

When we understand better how we unfolded through our childhood, we will find doorways that lead us back toward the wonder of our true being.

Our understanding doesn't have to be complicated. We don't have to take in overwhelming information; here in this book, my wish is to open a space for you, to share some reflections that may help you see beyond the thoughts of the intellectual mind.

Like each child's first welcome through the doorway of the school, we will begin in Chapter 1 with the safe space of acceptance, warmth, and care to lay our foundations, developing the strong roots that support us. And from there we can step into the world of imagination and possibility.

You will take in just what is needed, at your own pace. What speaks to you is exactly right for this time. Your exploration is to be honoured as unique.

You may read the book once and then revisit sections at different times. You may see things that were never before visible. The timing can be trusted.

This book is an overview of all that I have collected—a combination of learning, reflections, and experiences—on my own journey of understanding, and I am bringing it to you from where it moves me in my heart.

So take heart! I will show you where we are heading; you're not going to be led blindfolded into the pages of a long and tiring journey!

Rather, we are going on an adventure! An adventure of discovery and of nurturing new possibilities where you can stop and rest at any point. An adventure for you to meet yourself with so much love.

Our human journey of learning and understanding grows and moves in process as long as we are alive.

Our understanding is unique to each one of us, and our openness to see more creates endless possibilities.

From our willingness to open up, we can move beyond the fixed ideas of right and wrong, the agreement and disagreement of opinions, to try to understand more about each other, to make space for the "what if," to receive fresh perceptions at any moment.

THE
OVERVIEW

In Chapter 2, we'll look at the "Journey to Connection," naming and holding what gets in the way, and we'll also meet a truth about the power of our inner resources.

This chapter looks at the common struggles of our daily interactions, the search to find full attention and the trusting friendships we seek. In today's world, so many are asking, "Where is the real friend, the 'right' community, the people who understand? The people who speak their truth with love and kindness?"

We want to find people who genuinely believe in each other, people who are committed, with patience, to give the time and attention that seems to be lost in our busy, distracted lives.

Can a true listener be found who will hold space for you to allow your wisdom to come through in your speaking?

We pay lip service to honouring inner wisdom, yet we keep each other trapped or diverted with uncalled for advice, diversion from what feels too hard to face, and both conscious and unconscious manipulation.

We navigate life with a sense of being a separate being within our bodies, trapped in our own bubbles of belief, with the added weight of feeling misunderstood that deepens our suffering.

For many, the path to return to wholeness feels long. It can seem like an exhausting labyrinth of an endless assortment of therapies and programmes. Our emotions become tangled and complicated on a journey full of twists and turns, with detours that afterward feel unnecessary.

We choose one path, only to end up feeling that we are accountable to a perceived authority or that we are a failure for not meeting goals and targets.

We make other people into experts and gurus. We think we are not capable, that only this particular person can help, that *other people know so much more than I do.* We think it is easier to have someone else set the standards for our own lives.

Obligations and goals, either self-imposed or dictated by others, can feel heavy. "We're all in this together," people may tell us, but we can't feel it. Deep down, we feel fragmented, lost, and never quite enough.

The various self-development journeys we sign up for sometimes feel like one-way paths into darkness, and we still do not feel real compassion for ourselves. We return to the gnawing sense of dissatisfaction, feeling as though we have simply applied a temporary bandage with a new technique.

We are advised to practise more self-care—"love yourself more; you know you must"—yet the root cause of not loving ourselves is never really addressed. There is something we are overlooking, and we continue to feel less than whole.

We want to feel it. We read or listen to the words, we try hard, and still it hasn't yet sunk in. We want to believe it, to remember and trust that our understanding will unfold as it is meant: written in the stars, in the mystery of the universe and our place in it. It *sounds* amazing, we long for it, but it does *not feel* true.

In Chapter 3, we will step into a fresh place. We will put on new glasses to see things anew. While we were growing as little children, other people and the world were truly fascinating and wondrous.

The open, innocent perception that we once had may have become obscured as we were stopped in our tracks at certain points on our trusting childhood path.

I will open up a view of childhood experiences during three phases of development to show how, as children in our own stories, a sense of separation may have happened abruptly, before we were really ready and equipped to regulate ourselves.

In each phase, we will look at our universal human needs and the unique longings from our story in that particular phase.

Through imaginative recollection and sensory details, I want to help you not just understand these phases but *feel* them, to inhabit the child's world as a deep observer *and* as a participant, reconnecting to familiar situations to rediscover again the gifts of innocence and curiosity, the delight of new learning and being alive.

This process is not about nostalgic recollection or regret; it is about unlocking a deeper empathy for our own children today, in our roles of parent, grandparent, friend, or professional, whilst simultaneously rediscovering the parts of ourselves from our own childhood that we feel we have lost or denied in our adulthood.

By entering the heart of childhood, we can see the world with wonder, open to possibility, ever fresh, here and now.

In Chapters 4 and 5, I will guide you to discover the story of the parts. Throughout the miracle of our learning journey—with treasures always inherent like a map of learning—we see the design of our learning journey as a beautiful, emerging process from birth.

As children, our deepest wish is to be in connection with someone who loves us, sees us, and is willing to support us the best way they know how. We are born to connect, to reflect for each other the truth of who we are: whole, complete, and made of love.

It is in our DNA to seek each other out, to restore the life-giving benefits of connection throughout life. This is an innate drive, a passion in our being that is reflected in various expressions for each of us.

Did we receive this love, this devotion to our being, as we were growing?

Was it just enough?

Was there even a trace?

Is it too late?

Will we ever receive it?

I present an image for you:

We are born from oneness, our spirit entering a new physical body ready for life on earth. From our first moments, we seek reconnection as—now appearing contracted within human form—we yearn to remember our expansive nature.

Who ensured your warm and gentle welcome as you arrived on earth? From the moment of conception, as your physical form developed, warmth was essential for life to unfold.

In Chapter 6, I will share the vision of a warm and gentle welcome at birth—the precious, powerful beginning that uplifts us throughout our entire lives. I will create a gentle opening in your heart where we can recreate that welcome, sharing insights that illuminate the miracle of your being and the beauty of your origins.

This pivotal moment will prepare you to revisit the sacredness of your origin, allowing you to integrate this knowing into the wholeness of your being.

This book serves as a portal to your centre—where you feel truly at home—fostering a deep connection to the inner wisdom and peace that reside in the presence of your true nature.

We may not be consciously aware of the longings we carry in the background of our daily lives. We have not yet identified them, these longings rooted in the unmet needs experienced at particular times during our childhood years.

Through the sections of Truth, Beauty, and Goodness—each relating to the three phases of childhood—we discover what we are made of. These discoveries become the seeing of an open door.

We understand childhood not as one block of time in our life but as cycles of a special focus, each with their own particular needs and inherent gifts according to the awakening of our consciousness.

And from there, in our new opportunity—face-to-face in deep presence with the here and now—we allow these unconscious longings to speak to us, and we will see how to make each moment more alive and full.

From the time of the great philosophers, three important principles—Truth, Beauty, and Goodness—have been known. These are not just abstract ideas but reflections, pictures of our spiritual nature; they are the pillars that describe who we are, and as they are able to unfold they will lead us to a deeper understanding of ourselves and the world around us.

Truth, Beauty, and Goodness resonate deeply with us, reminding us of our connection and our unity with all the Universe.

- **Truth** helps us see things clearly.
- **Beauty** touches our hearts.
- **Goodness** teaches us to live with purpose and kindness.

As we grow, they become like invitations to awaken: truth in the body, beauty in the soul, and goodness in the spirit.

In Chapter 12, a new kind of listening lifts us up, a way of listening that becomes the centre of our lives, like the sunrise that keeps reminding us of who we truly are. How did we forget?

Now, in a new kind of listening—a listening that is filled with our directed attention, a listening to ourselves and to others, a listening to the truth, beauty, and goodness reflected in nature—we find hope. We immerse in the stillness of deep awareness, and it heals us, empowers us, and becomes a creative pathway to express love.

Beyond our names and roles, what is at the core? *Who is it? Who am I? Why am I here?* Every soul alive will ask these questions.

Reclaim the natural life forces gathered from each phase of childhood. Stay open to see the true beauty of your life. Hear your wisdom that has been lying so quiet, so patiently. This wisdom IS who you are; it was only forgotten.

Here, in this book, I invite you to come with me as I share what I have come to see is the only thing that matters: the tender, kind, patient places in connection that are waiting to lead both you and the other back to centre. It is through authentic, vulnerable connection, in warm presence and attention, that your heart softens and reconnects to the essence of your being.

Between hearts in this open, true connection, there is a kind of magic and warmth that lets in light—the light that opens understanding. Here in this sacred space, as we rest in presence, we become open to receiving the highest inspirations for our lives.

I invite you to journey with me. I can feel it is time.

Listen now. Do you hear it? It is a soft, persistent call back to yourself—to the wholeness you have always been.

From The Heart of Childhood

THE CALL BACK

"As we work to create light for others, we naturally light our own way."

~ Mary Anne Radmacher

Have you ever been in the presence of a soul companion? Do you know the sacred space of ones who hold you in unwavering faithfulness for the light that is waiting to shine within you?

What if we could bring in this energy for all those we encounter in our daily lives?

You are a soul companion. We are all soul companions to each other.

But in our hurry, we miss seeing the sacred light present in every human being. Perhaps it is hidden from our eyes, or perhaps we lost faith.

We have moved our focus, drawn away in the race to succeed or grasping at the image we think we need to make us happy, too caught up in the created "busyness" to see the sacred essence living at the core of each person.

The time has come to move beyond our familiar small circles, the exclusive spaces that, whilst they may help us feel safe may also keep us asleep and unchallenged.

We don't grow without staying open to the unknown. We need to feel how it is to open to a different view. For we are only here to see all of who we are, and we can do this for each other.

In every single meeting, every interaction, no matter in our limited perception how we rank the importance or value of the individual— from the most successful CEO to the seemingly insignificant delivery man, from the parent in charge to the tiny child, from the colleague to the friend—each human being has the capacity to share with and inspire us in their own unique way.

We are all connected, we are all human. We were all born from the same source.

"We are each someone because we are some of the One. We are each a masterpiece, a piece of the Master."
~Cathy Heller, *Abundant Ever After*.

For all the mothers—those who raise the next generation, the architects of the children's daily lives who hold such a great power in the world, the mothers who often feel empty, alone, exhausted, hoping to be seen as worthy and productive—they are torn and confused by the pull of their daily lives. They miss the true *seeing* of their children. They seek support, yet their relationships seem shallow. They are frequently caught in the uncomfortable space of comparison, veiled judgement, and envy.

For all the fathers—the partners who feel burdened by the weight of unspoken expectations and the culture of generations still living in the background of their lives, to "man up," be the "successful" provider or the "solution finder," and in this become fixed in their perceived roles, unseeing in the real support they are here to provide; those men who struggle to share their inner truth, avoiding vulnerability and the tender parts of themselves for fear of ridicule because they were once little boys in need of protection—they now, more than ever, need to know where they stand and feel the value of their true loving and powerful potential.

For the teachers—now disillusioned as the calling to teach has been drowned in the outcomes of the curriculum—no ears hear their passions, no eyes see their visions and hopes for the children.

For the solitary leaders and pioneers—the ones who manage teams, who must appear in control, efficient, and capable of motivation — many have lost connection to their own sense of being supported and understood. Maintaining apparent control, they become blind to the small acts of love and attention that are the bedrock of all the creations that are waiting to be brought to life.

For the writer, the artist, the healer—all those feeling alone and just "too different" in the creative space, the ones who feel they can only earn their living in conformity—no one is really present to hear their wildest, deepest creations. They inwardly live on the outer edges of the normal, accepted life.

For every soul alive on this earth:

We are *all* these things!

We hold these archetypes of our roles, these energies of the whole universe in our human experience.

And in our pain, we have a quiet connecting force that holds us together. In our shared humanity, we are all only searching to be understood, accepted, and seen as we move through the stories of our lives.

Underneath it all we are searching for the core of our shared essence, the same spirit that lives in each of us, soul-to-soul and heart-to-heart. We were born to seek out each other, with a passion that was planted in our souls.

From the earliest memories of childhood through the cycles of our growth, the stories of our lives shift and change. We face obstacles that must be overcome and people who come and go—fateful experiences and connections that shape who we are.

Would you like to feel the light of your soul every single day?

Do you want to understand how your unique gifts are needed?

The world is waiting, calling for what you have to offer.

I invite you now to uplift your connections, to welcome a new openness, allowing the greatest inspirations and insights to come to life.

To reclaim your inner presence, to bring your attention to another, to restore authentic connection—this is the greatest calling of our times.

We are here to be companions as we find our way to the inner strength and the inner ease that we are all searching for.

I am your companion in your truth seeking, here to walk with you; the holder of your space, here to move you from the scarcity of being heard in your raw essence to the expectation of soul companionship as your birthright.

In families, workplaces, schools, and communities, we have the power to heal and reignite connection to each other's magnificence.

What can we learn, what must we know, that will show us the way, that will bring us to the doorway of greater aliveness?

It is time to come into the tender space of loving presence. And so we begin with a warm and gentle welcome, creating a sanctuary where you can feel truly seen and heard—perhaps for the first time in many years. Let us step together into this space of reconnection, with a sigh of relief, where the path home to yourself awaits.

Your invitation is here. Push open the door when you arrive and walk right in . . .

CHAPTER 1

THE WARM AND GENTLE WELCOME

"I'm inviting Time inside.
offering a seat;
a room in my house so it can unpack its things.
letting It live with me
until all this tension I feel is relieved."

~ Abi Winder from HelloPoetry.com

COME INTO THE LISTENING SANCTUARY.

I am waiting at the doorway and I am just so glad you found your way here. Welcome! Come on in, let's go to the room with the fireplace and settle in.

Here is your warm drink, all the soft cushions, and a cosy blanket. Put up your feet, if you like, and sink into your deep armchair.

This room sings with a welcome. There are sparkling windows of softly filtered light, jewel-coloured flowers in a vase on the sill, a polished side table, the glow of a candle, the scent of lavender and sandalwood, a steaming teapot, all in the delight of your arrival.

I have so much I could share, heavy piles of books, long essays, and files of notes behind me on the bookshelves, quotes and techniques accumulated from long years of serious study.

Let us leave all these things where they are, on the shelf behind us. There is gratitude for the service of knowledge we have available, yet just now, these things are not needed.

Here we pause, we breathe out, we feel a sigh of relief, we arrive together.

By the soft flickering embers in the fireplace we see there are baskets of kindling at each side of the hearth for our fire.

We are held in the space we have created. I am so honoured to have you here with me. This is the space I prepared with love, in anticipation, holding you in my thoughts and looking forward to your arrival.

Take hold of your warm cup. Here, we can feel at ease. Here, you are free to make yourself at home. We will go at your pace.

No need to rush. I have time. This is our time.

Nowhere else to be right now.

We have come together to unite in the discoveries and experiences to be shared.

I offer up our space for you, for me, to allow whatever needs to come.

Welcome as you are, however you enter, at whatever stage you are feeling.

We are the writer and the reader.

The speaker and the listener.

Together, we create the space to say what needs to be said, to hear what must be heard, and to listen to the wisdom we find that is revealed between us.

THE PATH UNFOLDS

Now we have settled in, I will help to set a scene to make our beginning together.

Here you will find no long biography or deviation. I ask to share just what is needed, not a self-indulgent story but one that comes from those times that have most touched my heart—moments that feel now, as I remember and reflect back, to be like holders of wisdom for me, ready to be shared with you.

I find it extraordinary how events, people, and scenarios that played a part in life seem mysteriously connected, held by an invisible thread that brings us perfectly to the now.

I ask for courage to share what I have learned most recently—with nothing to prove and no one to please—as it comes to me at this moment.

I also believe you may recognize from this sharing a stirring within, a curiosity about the beautiful mystery of your own unique journey. Perhaps you'll feel encouraged to wonder a little more about moments and situations, some seemingly insignificant at the time, and those people who have come into your life, for you. I will be ready to listen whenever you wish.

Strangers yet to meet, already breathe within me
Invisible threads, silent as starlight
We arrive bearing gifts from souls who shaped our way
Though they never knew
Standing at the edge of now—looking back, looking forward
The thread never breaks.

A PASSION FOR WORDS

Here I am, just three years old, sitting in my mother's teacher chair in her classroom, my legs swinging high above the ground. And I am reading from a book—for the "going home" story—to a large class of tired, fidgety five-year-olds, as my mother reorganises and tidies the classroom at the end of the day. The children slowly begin to settle on the carpet around the chair.

I feel, in my barely three-year-old self, a pull to bring calm, a calling for balance, and an urge for deep caring, to soothe the overwhelm for us all in that overcrowded, exhausted, "end of the day" classroom. In the magic of the story, a retreat into the words held on the page, I feel complete trust; I have no sense of being in a spotlight as I have merged with the words. I am reminded of a magical world to which we all belong, with complete un-self-consciousness; it feels so natural to share.

I had begged to learn to read before even starting school, and I remember clearly it was the mysterious drawings in a particular storybook that drew me in, that sparked my desire to master what seemed so necessary for me: the illustrations of goblins underground and fairies perched in flowers, doorways, and gardens that led the way to stories that echoed within. I felt that there was magic in the pictures, and the words were the key to unlocking it. When I found the key to read the words I would be free to enter the world of the story for myself.

My childhood love of words for soothing and healing, for revealing a beauty that resonated within, has now become a conscious passion. I recognise the power of the art of language, of speaking and listening from a place held strongly in presence and awareness. Words can be powerful healers from the heart, or they can cause unconscious wounding to others and ourselves. Words can be a trigger of painful moments from the past when we lost connection with the true core essence of who we really are. And words can call in a resonance and lift us up, connecting us to the beauty and abundance that is ours.

A VARIED PATH

I left university in my early twenties, encountering the real world and asking myself, *What is a career? What is **my** career?* Of one thing I was certain: I would not be a teacher! I would not follow in the footsteps of my mother, my grandfather, my uncle, and my aunt!

Teaching, as was advised to me then, was a respectable job, practical, secure, safe, a steady income, convenient, and with school holidays too!

Growing up, as I witnessed the life of the teacher, I took in the sense of disillusionment, exhaustion, resentment, and scepticism of a disenchanted world.

On the brink of the age of adventure, I sought out instead what I felt was the wider exciting world: the bustle of the capital city, London, and the fascination of the mix of cultures.

My professional journey began in hospitality at a prestigious London hotel, where I learned the art of service with intuition, not from being formally taught but from sensing into and creating environments where subtle nuances, gesture, and comfort mattered. Working with demanding VIP guests taught me how to remain grounded while attending to the wild needs of restless souls.

Next, as a recruitment consultant, I navigated the delicate balance between authentic connection and professional expectations, witnessing firsthand the tension between genuine human matching and the pressure of weekly sales targets.

My path then led me, with my fiancé, to Hong Kong, where I became a temporary preschool teacher. Though my legs finally reached the floor from the teacher's chair, I felt humbled by the confident expertise of my colleagues as I entered the mysterious world of young children. But then, I no longer lived in the world of the child, as I was now a self-conscious adult. I was curious, though I felt exposed, unknowing, vulnerable.

When I was newly married, I moved away from the teaching that I had declared I would never do. Believing I needed a "proper career," I ventured from the "lowly" classroom into Hong Kong real estate—a competitive, ego-driven environment of cutthroat deals and backstabbing dynamics. Despite my efforts to adapt to its rhythms, I felt deeply disconnected—an outsider desperately trying to belong. I was merely performing, like a fish out of water, unable to identify the essential element missing within myself.

The pivotal return to the classroom came as we contemplated starting our own family. What I discovered there was a deep revelation—the world of the wise child, whose pure energy and innocent wisdom far exceeded my own.

In this next seemingly simple preschool setting, away from the glamour and competition, I encountered the profound gifts hidden in early childhood—treasures not yet understood that would gradually shape my understanding of authentic connection and the transformative power of presence. For this is what it seemed the children openly expected. It was both a healing and a seeing of the discord and discontent of the frantic adult world.

It was a world that required courage, I would see, this world of the child. There was plenty to challenge me in my learning and becoming, a new kind of seeing with new eyes to witness a gradual emerging of each soul just beginning a powerful journey—the child's pure energy shining a light on who I was—around the children who embodied more innocent wisdom than I could ever imagine. And I started to wake up and see that my deepest learning to date had begun!

My working life and the questions that arose from these experiences and encounters began to shape me further. I became a mother—a mother who dived headfirst, submerged in such great visions for her own children, never to be the same—to everything brand new, carrying my role models within, deciding how to parent.

THE SACRED RAGE

"Let the flame of anger free you of all falsity."

~ John O'Donohue, "For Presence"

On a humid, sticky morning, we climbed the three flights of the narrow stone stairway together, my little two-year-old girl trustingly holding my hand. We entered the small, crowded classroom.

A group of children were being led in a guided activity at the painting table. The teacher was preoccupied, and she was frowning. The children were eerily quiet. The room felt regimented and not alive. I felt strangely as though I was an inconvenience, unwelcome and in the way. I smiled, trying to break the ice, feeling apprehensive. And then I was asked to leave my child quickly. It was for the best, I was told.

And so began the traumatic start at school as my daughter was forcibly separated from me on her very first day.

I left the room, confused but obedient whilst she cried, objected, and called for me. She cried herself into an exhausted sleep to shut out the agony. She did not understand, she could not understand; it was an unnatural and fearful situation—a strange place with people she did not know and no concept of when I would return.

She was still asleep when I came back, the reflexes of her body still gulping in air. Even as I write this, I feel both the shame at my ignorance and the aching in my heart for her, for me. I was caught off guard. I felt pressured to conform and obey the "teacher" and the expectations. I had left her there and then returned home to feed her newborn baby brother.

I was told by another visiting parent, one that was considering an assistant role, that my daughter had been scraping at the door of the nursery classroom, but the main teacher had instructed the assistant teachers not to comfort her—the "abandoned child."

I, the sleep-deprived young mother with a colicky new baby, had lost touch with my inner knowing. I had no anchor. I was completely overwhelmed. I was unable to access my own wisdom, to be the advocate, the protector that I now so wish I had been able to bring forth from inside.

I felt the swirl of the feelings of unworthiness and betrayal coloured by my own previous unconscious needs and lack: *Listen to the "expert." Who do you think you are to think you know better?*

I felt that familiar human thought: not good enough, failing in my role as a mother, becoming stuck in a programmed place in my mind that dictated, "Never repeat this. Avoid any similar situation at all costs. And remember all the details."

What can be so easy to judge from the outside must be understood from the inside. Do we really know what is going on for someone else? We try to look at the facts, but from our own view, without support we always add our own interpretation. As individual human beings, we each have our own experience of the same situation from within the bubble of our own existence.

This seemingly "little" story connects me to so many mothers here and now who feel shame, exhaustion, unsupported, and closed off from their own inner knowing.

Looking back now, I see how I, as the young mother, perhaps needed my own advocate and protector—the wise woman of the tribe—to nurture me, to listen, to help me find my truth, to remind me of my own knowing, to give me some rest that was so sorely needed! I needed the me of the now back then!

For my daughter, this memory remains blurred. I have asked her about it now that she is a mother herself, yet in those early years of her life she was without her developed capacity to process the experience in the still forming part of her rational mind. She is now not certain what this memory contains for her, although I remember the patience and time needed to develop her trust in being left in a school setting again!

We may brush off the unconscious lingering effects in adulthood, when we can't access the facts or even much of the memory, but the experience is held in the body and will always be knocking, calling for our attention—expressed in various ways—until it is comforted, listened to, and held and healed.

In this situation I have just described, I did not know—could not reflect or ponder a possibility—that the teacher in charge of my daughter's fateful first nursery school also had stuck beliefs and strategies. I acted from my default system. I imagine her default system was telling her, *Crying is bad. Control the behaviour. A child must toughen up—be ready for school. Your job as an adult is to "teach a lesson."*

I was afraid of this teacher; it was an unconscious memory, a conditioning from my own childhood.

This adult teacher, I can now see better but could not understand then, had ideals and beliefs that came from a cycle perpetuated from her own childhood experiences, from her own adult role models. She had also been conditioned in her earlier life. This teacher, placed in such a role, was deeply disconnected from her own natural love and wisdom.

What did she not receive in her own childhood?

Where was her role model for care, attention, and compassion to teach her so she could embody these qualities and comfort a distressed child?

As my first two children approached kindergarten age, I knew I could not rely on the type of preschool environments I had seen. I could not choose them just because there was nothing else. It was competitive. It was business-oriented and conflicted in educational motives.

After the shock, I felt a slow but passionate anger rising, a healthy anger—a sacred rage—I see now in a way that stirred me to action, that pointed me toward a calling. I felt deeply that there had to be something better.

If no one could create a nurturing preschool experience for children so young, then I would do it. I would create a home away from home, a gradual transition and bridge! It would be a place where parents were not immediately excluded, a place of a big, warm, gentle welcome, where healthy relationships between children and parents were respected and regarded as vital, and where caring adults—those important secondary attachment figures—would help children feel safe.

Children need to feel and be given the chance to experience attuned connections, the foundation for their ability to know and feel into self-regulation for the future. I had a very clear vision. Here was a new powerful energy.

THE SCHOOL OF LIFE

Spurred on by supportive friends (and thanks to my ex-boss at the estate agency!), and along with two like-minded mothers, with the intention of opening a school, I was able to rent a characterful house opposite the beach. The large, black, wrought iron gates gave it the name: Highgate House School.

My vision was to create a place of safety—a nurturing, sensitive, safe holding space (thanks to the hospitality lessons at the London hotel!)—where play and imagination would take centre stage alongside artistic activity.

We had access to the beach, and a garden with sand, soil, and water. I joined forces with these two other mothers for administration and for sharing a passion for a curriculum. I enrolled in play-based teacher training, drew from my other experiences in my early teaching career, and began crafting a curriculum that came from the heart.

I didn't find it an easy journey. There were ups and downs, of course, and so much to be learnt. I had to overcome a great fear of speaking up and addressing large groups. I became the spokesperson to fight for the need for this preschool and, loaded with caffeine (not sure how helpful that was!), I presented to a boardroom of town planners.

In search of those who shared a deep care for and devotion to childhood, I interviewed teachers (thanks to the practice in the recruitment chair!), seeking out those who genuinely connected to and felt called to support the early childhood stage.

Almost immediately, from the very first week of opening, families began knocking at the door. They, too, were ready to break the mold of the competitive and inappropriate offerings elsewhere.

All went well, and after the arrival of our third child—our second son—and just before the handover of HK back to China in 1997, we moved temporarily to the UK. I was still closely connected to the running of Highgate House, and we travelled frequently back and forth across the world.

Whilst in the UK, I enrolled in a part-time postgraduate teaching course in Montessori Education. With three children and a new lifestyle, I refurbished the outbuildings of our home, designing and opening another small nursery and kindergarten set in a beautiful natural woodland. Here was the space for our third child to go to preschool. And there amid that setting, our fourth child was born.

But we did not stay. Something else was calling. We moved house again, seemingly randomly; there was no reason other than we wanted to downsize and we were attracted to a particular house. It had good vibes, rambling gardens, enchanting history, and beautiful windows. It was close to the village of Forest Row, East Sussex. It was there I encountered Rudolf Steiner's anthroposophy—meaning "wisdom of the human being"—in Michael Hall School and the famous Emerson College for teacher training, in addition to all sorts of other wonderful courses that ensued.

I was immediately touched right within my heart by the reverence for the child in the magical story like classrooms of the kindergarten and the deep understanding of our human developmental journey. I was searching, wondering, excited, and inspired by great information and new learning.

Going all in over the next decade—it now feels like a whirlwind of challenge, between travelling, raising children, moving and renting homes in HK, renting out our UK home, renting other homes many times, consulting and supporting other school founders—I explored and studied play therapy, adult counselling, and parent-group facilitating.

In my full-on early mothering years, there was an energy that wanted to go toward all that I was to be for my children as they grew and as I learnt about child development in depth and what it was to become a mother to my own family.

The irony was that I started preschools *for them*, and yet with the long hours of study and practice required in the courses, and busyness running the schools, I began to feel I was missing opportunities of connection at home. This is where more longings came in that started to shape who I was to become.

I often returned to the same question, asking inwardly, *what is this mothering I am here to do? What should mothers do?* And then I would keep trying the best I knew how (as we all do), stumbling along, making mistakes, experiencing moments of both great joy and also desperation, worry, isolation (*who understands me?*), restlessness, and always searching for more . . .

I look back now and long for more of the quiet pause moments and slower connection points when I could make space to just *be* and to fully enjoy connection time with each child. I could not allow myself this "luxury," as I saw it. There were things to prove, places to be.

It is time that I wish, in hindsight, I could get back, a kind of wistful, sad yearning that so many parents will realise over the years after childhood is suddenly over.

And I hear the older, wise woman's voice that warns us how fast it goes. As my own grandmother used to say, "Enjoy it now. Slow down a little." How strange I find it now becomes my own voice telling others!

Eventually, we can come to understand the bigger picture: we come to understand that the time is always *now*.

It is here in a redirection back to presence: to acknowledge and hold the longings and bring loving attention to them so they can be thanked for the lessons and the messages and allowed to rest. It is now that we can begin fresh each moment.

We need to remind each other of this! Regularly! This is the beauty and purpose of our connections: to delight in life, to be strengthened in presence.

Here, where we are, is where we can make the difference. And sometimes, this truth can be heard more clearly in the vulnerable, authentic space of real connection.

And our children need us to see them *as* they are, *where* they are, not living in the past in regret, not worrying and projecting constantly into the future nor trying to keep and remember them as they once were in our favourite times when we seemed to have control, when they were "ours."

In 2001, I returned to Hong Kong with our two youngest (the two elder children started boarding at secondary school), so I could bring deeper insights into the curriculum to expand to larger premises with more outdoor space and create new parent and child groups.

It was not an easy decision to return full time to Hong Kong, but there was a sense that something had to shift in our lives. My husband felt a calling back to Hong Kong and decided to join me and support me in bringing new life to the school. He sensed my passion for the curriculum and shared a desire to contribute something meaningful to the children of his home city.

I did feel inspired and energised to bring teacher training and parent education classes—connected to a wish for children to be given more time to grow their roots and for parents, teachers, and caregivers to be supported, knowing that helping them is really truly helping the children. Ironically my heart also ached for our two children going to boarding school. They both did not want to return to HK. It was a turning point and an awakening for us both as parents.

I worked closely on a UK-recognised Steiner Waldorf teacher training course adapted for HK; I called it "Conscious Teaching." There was no such previous training in HK. I placed the emphasis on self-development for adults as an ongoing, open self-enquiry: a new view of childhood and a better understanding of children's needs to see how closely who we are reflects and resonates into our children.

Looking back, I can see more clearly what has led me to this point of wanting to share now, in a quieter yet more grounded way, all the things that inspired me.

As we listen to another person's stories, there is an invitation to open ourselves up a little more, to create space for new insights as we walk through the pictures of situations and hear of the challenges that have influenced a life.

There is a feeling, in hindsight, of being quietly guided, led by a powerful benevolence, even when at the time we do not understand why certain things happened that often that felt out of our control.

My thoughts, my hopes, and the essence of this book grew from all these learnings and teachings, nourished further through deep conversations with two dear colleagues. The three of us have shared special moments together over the years, learning to practice listening in a new way. Through our ongoing dialogue—voices coming together, always in process—we discovered truths about connection and presence that transcended what any of us could have found alone.

INSPIRATIONS

Three together—a magical number—playfully calling ourselves Witches of Westwick (WOW!), were led by our fierce passion for childhood and parenting, love of the arts and the deep learning of all adults who live around children.

We concocted "potions" and remedies in our "cauldron." We shared deep conversations around the office desks in the container of the school for situations that came our way, moving between our heads and our hearts, into wonderings and imaginations as we practised our listening. Our questions always returned to, "How can we serve, what have we come to do, and what is it each one of us can bring?"

We helped each other with commitment and awakening gratitude for the insights we received together.

I have come to see the spiritual power in true shared decision-making, the miracle of guided inspirations created through our willingness to set aside the small ego and truly listen—listen so we can hear what is waiting to be heard.

I am dedicated to remaining open and interested in truth that has no dogma, that is experienced in real life, always in process of understanding, and felt and known by our spirit.

A NEW SURRENDER

And a woman who held a babe against her bosom said,
Speak to us of Children.
And he said:
Your children are not your children.
They are the sons and daughters of Life's longing for itself.
They come through you but not from you,
And though they are with you yet they belong not to you.
You may give them your love but not your thoughts,
For they have their own thoughts.
You may house their bodies but not their souls,
For their souls dwell in the house of tomorrow, which you cannot visit, not even in your dreams.
You may strive to be like them, but seek not to make them like you.
For life goes not backward nor tarries with yesterday.
You are the bows from which your children as living arrows are sent forth.
The archer sees the mark upon the path of the infinite, and He bends you with His might that His arrows may go swift and far.
Let your bending in the archer's hand be for gladness;

*For even as He loves the arrow that flies, so He loves
also the bow that is stable.*

~ Kahlil Gibran, "On Children" from *The Prophet*

I often wished I could have had more time with my eldest two children, wondering how the teenage years passed by so quickly as they changed and grew and became young adults in the spaces between our visits and during the family holidays as we crossed halfway around the world so many times in a year.

And then time moved us into another era: the wondrous birth of a baby boy—our daughter gave birth and we were blessed with our first grandchild!

When my daughter became a mother herself, something powerful shifted within me. Standing by the stark hospital incubator, taking in my first glimpse of my grandson, I whispered a gentle welcome. Then a nurse came to tell me to not stay too long. Again, I had a sense that she did not want the inconvenience to accommodate a visitor. There was nothing seriously wrong with my grandson, and there was only one other baby sleeping peacefully at the other end of the large room. I felt a new voice rising inside me—a calm yet fiercely protective voice of the grandmother that I had envisioned myself becoming. And I stayed by that incubator to take the time as I welcomed this new little life.

In the clinical space of the hospital, watching my own daughter now become a mother herself, I witnessed a profound transition happening across our family. This tiny being hadn't just created new parents; he had awakened two grandparents, and the grandmother instinct that had been waiting in me instantly came alive.

I found myself wanting to become a bridge: supporting my brave daughter as she faced overwhelming new challenges, responsibilities, and choices, encouraging my determined son-in-law as he stepped into a more engaged fatherhood than previous generations had known, and most importantly, becoming a steady presence for this new little person who had joined our family.

Something fundamental shifted in that moment by the incubator—the natural desire to hold space, offer guidance, and be in service to these three precious lives now connected in a new way through me, through my husband, linking our family's past to its future through this tender present moment.

My early memories of my own maternal grandmother sparked love; she was kind and patient and had an unparalleled ability to listen to me. Until I was a teen at least, then it became another story—her story, our entangled generational story—and then it was more difficult for us both.

I envisioned myself as a wiser, more reflective woman, an "Elder," destined to become a stronger anchor for the family and to extend that support into the community. I wanted to be a companion, a guide, a secure base of both passionate and tender love for a mother's task and her child's new awakening. I wanted to be a grandmother firmly rooted in the calm presence of her being—a real grandmother.

There is the ideal vision and then there is the down-to-earth, real human messy experience—the challenges of our daily existence. In the reality of daily life, I wanted to pass on what I had gathered, but I also needed to learn how to empower wisdom in others—the most important lesson for me to learn being: when to speak and when to be silent; when to act and when to let go, to discern what is true help; what is my need derived from my own sense of lack, and how to find a balance, to be compassionate with others and to feel compassion for myself.

And what was also awakened was a sense that society's view of the older woman who is "no longer relevant" would not become a definition for me.

I moved into a vulnerable place—a place of deep longings, of aching heart, of ideas that I wanted to share—but felt called to listen more, testing out the roles from a place of letting go, learning to allow, surrender, and realise that the learning never stops.

And then soon to follow, another grandson!

The miracle of a new birth brings fresh energy and attention from a different perspective. New life brings renewal. Now that beautiful poem by Khahil Gibran touched me more deeply than before. I re-read the words from a different place in my body, heart, and mind.

I learned the art of surrendering, of loving not out of my own need to nurture and be wanted and needed but out of pure recognition of the love to set free a spiritual being and honour a unique destiny.

Drops of Joy

The rain began falling, large drops on the balcony railing,
Gentle and glistening in beams of sunlight filtering through mist.
He was in my arms, so new to the world
His trusting body relaxed and soft.
We both have the gift of time
And in that timeless bubble,
One wondrous word,

"Rain."
I held out my hand just to the edge,
and the raindrops landed on my upturned hand.
I looked at him, he looked at me
Eyes of awe, Eyes of wonder
He smiled, I smiled
The smile of the resonance
The dance of the hearts.
"Raindrops," I said.
Savouring a new word,
I looked upwards and into the sky as his eyes also opened wider.
A synaptic moment
Just this moment . . . all that is needed.
The forever moment
The attunement
A recognition of the fresh beauty of the world
And our place in it, Together.

I felt my heart expanding, feeling more joy, yet also more calm, feeling a presence and also more connected to the sense of a pull, a connection belonging to beauty—all called in by new life. A love so strong for this new life, I recognised it deep inside.

The love is a gift that brought me closer to the space of wonder, to open up a deeper connection to all of life.

Yes, the childhood journey in hindsight seems to pass by so quickly, and I came to know through experience, to recognise deeply in the challenge, that returning to presence, to ease at its centre, will reveal for us all that is needed.

Here in this moment was a connection between us—with nature, with the simple rain—uniting us in such a profound and utterly beautiful way.

How to allow, how to protect, how to love?

How to be the stable force, knowing you are made of love, so that you can be there for another? So that you can bring all that magnificence of love to light up another?

It is time to bring an evolution of love.

I sense deeply within my soul that the childhood journey will show us the way; for every soul alive has a child within.

In the meeting of another being, experienced in the sacred innocence, in wisdom carried through time, full in the shining spirit of a new child—we all are looking for this "tuning in" to each other. I see you. And I see you see me. This energy is a gift and a deep experience that can pass between two beings.

Whether a baby or a fully grown adult, it is the same pure spirit, the same core.

We are seekers yearning to tune in to the subtle frequencies of our human souls. When we meet in the space between our hearts, whether in the innocent gaze of a child or the weathered eyes of an older person, there is a profound transmission.

From the drops of joy we encounter with children, there is the chance for a sacred moment of mutual recognition where boundaries dissolve to open us up and outward. We begin to understand that in our quest to truly see one another, we look through lenses clouded by experience, judgement, and assumptions.

What if we could return to that pure state of perception we once knew as children—before we learned to categorize, before we built walls from our hasty judgements?

In the next chapter, I describe a view of our human experience in seeking connection.

To face and embrace our blocks and fears takes courage, and it is our first step—a powerful first step! To pause there, in the discomfort, is our brave space. We usually do not allow anxiety and fear to sit with us, and we don't take the time to hear what they have to say, believing we must get rid of them or dismiss them before they bring us down.

From this place of holding and acknowledging, of witnessing and not rejecting, we'll discover how a doorway opens. Here we find there is no effort needed; we breathe in deeply and we breathe out slowly, and we allow; we bring a gentle attention that opens a profound release and renewal.

CHAPTER 2

THE JOURNEY FOR CONNECTION

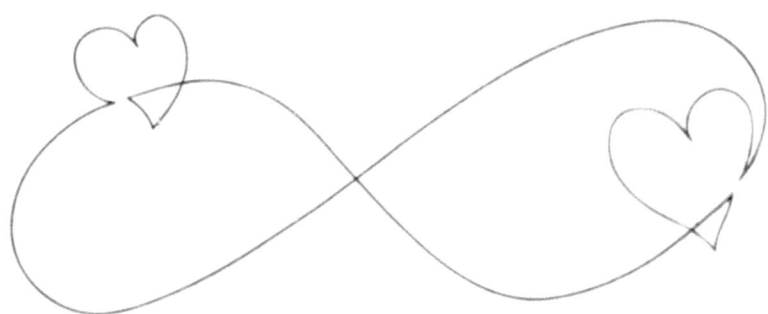

<u>Sacred Encounters</u>

Here she is, in the magical space of her grandmother's garden,
Encircled safely by the rustling green of boundary hedges.
There are little openings, shapes between the leaves.
Pockets of light filter through, and glimpses of the pavement
along the street outside.

A whole other world expands wondrously out into the not yet
known.
People, people are walking by!
Some catch sight of the curious, wide open eyes peering through
the hedge.
Some scurry on by, and some stop,
Pause and smile.
Her heart bubbles with delight and joy.
Other people!
"Hello you, who is that little girl in the hedge there?!"
They bend down, gently moving aside the leaves.
"Hello! It's me! I am 3 years old. I'm just playing here,
My grandma is in the kitchen. Where are you going?"
Innocent words, no filters,
and the words speak unhindered from Speech itself.
The kind lady, the kind man,
They tell her the little things about themselves.
Who else wants to listen with so much warm curiosity?
For this moment, there is just this,
A moment in time.
Stop, wait, watch, listen
Intimate connection, a pulsing heart,
Sparks dancing through the hedge each way,
Exchanged in the beauty of the Sacred Encounter.

There was a natural joy in our early childhood conversations when people gave us their time, echoed our warm interest and exchanges of the heart no matter the age.

As young children, we lived free from judgement or criticism in our thoughts and language. Everyone seemed fascinating to us. We didn't know how to cleverly manipulate conversations or hide behind carefully chosen words. Instead, we were completely genuine, like open books, expressing whatever emerged from our developing hearts and minds with pure authenticity. Our communication flowed directly from our true selves, unfiltered and honest.

Our souls seek another person, to understand and get to the heart of their being. A natural expression, when filled with an interest that has a warm energy and when the space inside of us can open without fear, is to encounter another and let them in.

Throughout our lives, we seek authentic connection because we know in that precious, focussed, open, vulnerable space created between you and me, there is an exchange that goes beyond our words. We no longer feel isolated, and there is joy in a recognition of our shared being.

What happened to us? The essence of who we really are perhaps went unseen, was rejected or ignored, at various points on our childhood journey. As we grew, our attempts at forming connections with others may have been missed or even ridiculed. With repeated experiences of rejection many of us became programmed to avoid further pain. Isolation, distraction, and avoidance, amongst other behaviours, were the coping mechanisms.

We now don't recognize how we've become trapped in our accumulated beliefs and survival patterns. These patterns aren't just mental constructs—they're stored physically in our cells and embedded in the unconscious, instinctual parts of our minds.

THE BARRIERS WE BUILD

We avoid the pain of failed relationships by not relating on a deeper level; it's too risky now, so we create and perpetuate that lonely bleakness by trying to appear and stay in control, to be independent and strong, to create a barrier of protection. And we become very contracted within ourselves, unwilling to show vulnerability. It feels far too threatening, so we stay safe; our automatic survival is a looping circuitry in our minds that repeats whenever we sense our defenses are threatened.

When we've searched and searched, trying to find someone who can hold our safety, and everyone falls short, we find ourselves saying, "I'll just do it alone." We have secretly given up, believing we no longer need anyone, or we create different false personas, adapting as we need in our search for recognition by others.

In the overwhelm of our lives we feel incredibly lucky when we experience exchanges with another from the heart of our true being, when (or if) we find that one person with enough focussed time for us.

As adults, the compassionate voice in our own centre, the one connected to wisdom and inspiration, feels far out of reach. Another person who listens to truly understand can help us come back to ourselves and to this place of compassion.

Yet, if listening is so powerful then why is it so hard? Why can we not slow down enough to become truly open and curious about ourselves or another?

Genuine human connection can be overshadowed by the many shallow, guarded interactions we fall into creating, the surface relationships that fail to hit the spot because they don't enter into the deep heartspace—our heart space that we so closely protect, and yet that so longs to be filled.

We keep trying to bring our attention, and yet we frequently feel we are failing.

We are manipulated by the media and unconsciously trapped in a search for comfort, reassurance, and validation. Our sense of satisfaction is always just out of reach or felt as a barely fleeting moment of fulfilment.

We feel there is never enough time, and our days are crammed with to-do lists. We keep creating these endless lists fuelled by the energies of consumption, comparison; we are distracting and protecting ourselves from the fear of feeling pain.

> *"I will not cause pain without allowing something new to be born."*
>
> **~ Isaiah 66.9**

THE PATH TO HEALING AND RECONNECTION

The crucial first step is to honestly identify and acknowledge our current state; to meet ourselves exactly where we are, without judgement.

We do not heal the pain by avoiding or denying the lack, the emptiness, the ache of disconnection but by allowing it to gently show itself. This is a courageous first step. We breathe and give it time. We ask what might it need, with warmth and soft curiosity.

In this energy we connect to the pain so that it is held, opening our heart a little more so that it can show us the message it wanted to give us. When we become more present with it, it may or may not at this time, be dissolved. We ask simply to bring more light and we invite new perceptions with our openness.

I promise if we take the time, we will feel relief in naming it, embracing it, and it will certainly move within us. From out of the stuckness, the body knows what it needs to do.

We need to reveal to be able to heal.

There is hope that when we open our eyes and hearts with compassion for our challenging situations, each one of us will find a recognisable human struggle.

We crave the connections where trust opens, where our voice speaks freely, where we have each other's best interest in our hearts. We all search to be seen, but at the same time we are so afraid of revealing what is really inside.

"Your task is not to seek love but merely to seek and find within you all the barriers that you have made to block it, and embrace them."

~Rumi

So, here we go. Let's begin to find and name those recognisable human obstacles that we struggle with. What is it like for us living in these times? Let us just lay it all out. Let us see more clearly and look honestly at how it really feels.

There is no need to pretend or to protect. Take a pause, slow down, and breathe.

THE IMPACT OF CHILDHOOD WOUNDS AND UNMET NEEDS

At different stages of childhood, particular needs were formed. These unmet needs remain conscious or unconscious, stuck in the developmental stage where they originally emerged.

In response to the need, we develop a longing and so we are driven unconsciously to look to others to fulfill what remains unresolved within ourselves. As our inner child is stuck in the stage, we are unconsciously searching for the adult we needed then, to fulfil the sense of lack we feel now.

As adults, it becomes so hard to understand what has gone wrong because our memory is locked in our primitive survival brain, and it feels as though we are bound in heavy chains. We can be triggered at the most inconvenient times.

As adults, we may have a constant need for attention, reassurance, or nurturing. Maybe you'll also recognise the following traits:

Being on edge or defensive, quick to assume the worst in others or lash out, even when people are just being "normal."

Always feeling let down, constantly disappointed by life, people, or situations no matter what actually happens.

Taking rejection too hard, getting much more upset than makes sense when someone criticizes you or says no.

People-pleasing overdrive, trying too hard to make everyone like you, hiding your real self in the process.

Cutting moral corners, ignoring or feeling disconnected from the inner voice that tells you right from wrong, leading to dishonest or unethical choices and behaviour.

These unmet needs stem from experiences where love and physical care was conditional, or where as a child we were forced to grow up too quickly without the necessary emotional support. There is fear and a sense of sadness that we have been abandoned.

THE SILENT TREATMENT

One aspect of disconnection that has touched me very deeply is the experience of being deliberately ignored. To be excluded, cast out, or humiliated out of the circle of care—falling from favour with a loved one and feeling unworthy of belonging—ranks for many among the most painful and fearful of human experiences.

This rejection can activate the primal wound of abandonment, whether emotional or physical. We carry this pain of disconnection from our earliest childhood experiences, with each new rejection reopening and deepening old wounds.

If we did not experience the embrace of a warm welcome at our birth, we are even more vulnerable. We can feel that we are nowhere in the mind of another person, even when we are physically right there, and we begin to feel unworthy or insignificant if this experience was repeated regularly when we were children.

We may then transfer the impact of our pain onto another. We can be so concerned with our own sense of missing self that we have no space inside to notice another. Lost in our own bubble, this kind of blindness to or ignoring of another can be either unconscious or deliberate.

The silent treatment isn't simply withholding words—it can be like an act of revenge or punishment. When someone deliberately cuts off communication, there's often a belief that the "offender" deserves to feel the same hurt the punisher feels, or must learn a lesson through the enforced isolating experience.

Being deliberately ignored creates a profound sense of having been erased. I've found myself wondering, *Where have I gone? Do I even exist?* This invisibility is devastating—and I recognize the painful pattern of both choosing relationships where this happens and inflicting it on others.

It's important to distinguish this punitive silence from the silence that is a gift—that sacred space where inner wisdom can be heard. A loving, kind silence can be restorative, gentle, and patient—a full container holding reverence for the other. This form of silence nurtures connection, unlike the silent treatment that cuts us off.

Moments adults might dismiss as insignificant can deeply etch patterns into developing minds of children, shaping future reactions, actions, and state of being. The early protective strategies we created, while once necessary, ultimately prevent true connection with others. The younger we were when these unhelpful patterns formed, the more profoundly they seem to impact our future relationships.

We can wake up to this as parents, as our children are always demanding from us that we bring our whole true self. They come with an expectation. They have an innate knowing that pulls them toward authenticity, as we all do throughout our lives.

PROJECTION AND ILLUSION

We transfer our unmet longings and needs onto other people, projecting onto them the ideal version of *the one* who will finally see us. Our hopes persist, and momentarily we are joyful, happy that here, at last, we have found what we were looking for: the *one*, the *thing* that we needed. But what we desperately seek—the image we have conjured up—disappears as we draw closer, and we find we are grasping at an illusion created from our own sense of incompleteness.

At first, we put *the one* on a pedestal; they can do no wrong! Such joy that all will be well, for this is the person I have been waiting for! And then . . . tragedy strikes as, sooner or later, they fall off, it seems without warning. Some trivial ordinariness or irritating habit, the starkness of humanity, makes the pedestal crumble and the illusion fade in the light of day.

We did not know we made them the means of filling our emptiness—a fabricated relationship that we hoped would heal our wounds. Hopeful expectations are dashed again. Our wondrous, once "shining saviour"—the love of our life, the expert we worship—becomes another frustrating and annoying obstacle in the path. When fragile humanity is revealed, we are disappointed in the imperfection of the human that reflects back at us.

The one does not meet the mark as we are brought back to the belief that shaped us—the idea of "not good enough"—and he or she does not really understand us and has broken the unspoken rules. We do not realize that the lack of kindness, the cruelty, or the perceived ignorance from the other stems from the same pain we feel. The other is not free to be who *they* really are. The other is also in chains.

If I could remember this, how would my perception change?

THE PATTERNS WE CAN'T SEE

When we hold on to our fixed beliefs about who we are, we cannot see the truth. We blame, criticise and judge. This is our default when we are triggered, and the pain from the childhood experience digs deep.

We feel dominated and unsettled by the discomfort of constant comparison. Envy is seen as normal, even to be used as a common motivator for progress, especially in media and marketing.

Criticism is overt or disguised as advice and stems from deep fear that the difference I sense in you threatens my very being. "Reject my advice, and you reject me!"

If only we could find reverence and awe for each other all the time.

Why doesn't it last?

Why do we repeatedly fall into disappointment and disdain?

And so here we are. We have arrived at this place inside that wants our attention.

THE FORGOTTEN GIFT OF FULL ATTENTION

Have you ever felt the weight of distraction pressing down on you? That moment when you're sitting across from someone, but your mind is anywhere but *here*? Most of us will have an experience of this: glancing sideways at our phones, watching the clock, feeling an inexplicable urge to be somewhere else. Perhaps there is a pang of guilt. We try to look interested. We think it's working for a second, maybe the other doesn't know. But deep down we both know, in our core, the conversation will miss the mark.

Our world has become a landscape of constant interruption. We've built walls of digital noise, creating a false sense of connection that leaves us more alone than ever. When was the last time you truly listened? Not just heard words, but really listened to another person's soul?

We are afraid of silence, terrified of boredom. We fill every moment with meaningless talk, convinced that empty space is something to be feared.

What if those quieter slower moments are where real connection begins? Moments of silence are a gift for ourselves to connect deeper, and for the other where we meet in the space that just for now needs no words.

Our fears drive us. We fear being controlled, so we control. We fear being misunderstood, so we hide. We push away painful feelings, creating a cycle of distraction that promises safety but delivers only emptiness. Our minds, once designed to protect us, now trap us in an endless loop of disconnection.

We can also sense that the world has changed rapidly through the kind of false connection we have created through technology and social media. Many of the daily in-the-flesh connections of our traditional social interactions are replaced with online meetings or artificially composed emails. It is also harder to distinguish the subtleties, and the feelings conveyed through the body of the characters on the screen, if we are to understand and connect to the deeper aspects in our encounters.

Our conversations tend to become transactions: timed, efficient, goal-oriented. We worry about wasting time, about not appearing productive enough. We've forgotten that the most profound connections often happen in moments with no clear purpose, when we simply allow ourselves to be present.

There is another way.

This isn't about rejecting technology or returning to some idealized past. It's about rediscovering the art of presence. Of listening beyond words. Of seeing the entire person, not just the carefully curated image they present.

We open in this moment to allow our full, vulnerable self to speak to us, quietly within. We can give ourselves complete attention.

From this more centred place we then have a choice to move our attention out to another. Here, something magical happens. We create a space where healing can begin, where understanding can grow. We no longer need to pretend. We no longer need to adapt or change, just to fit in and belong.

In times of overwhelm, the most beautiful connections are forged when we allow someone to truly see us, not as the perfectly presented curated self but in all our humanity, as we are. When we bear witness to each other's suffering. When we set aside our defenses and simply be.

Our attention is a gift. It cannot be forced. We can choose it, yet it can only be given freely, with love and openness.

As Henry Miller wrote in *Black Spring*,

"The moment one gives close attention to anything, even a blade of grass, it becomes a mysterious, awesome, indescribably magnificent world in itself."

Giving full attention is love in its purest form—a surrender to this moment, to ourselves, to each other.

A LIBERATING WISDOM, A HEALING PATH

As we explore the three phases of childhood development, we will start to feel a new awareness opening. We may begin to recognize patterns in our adult lives that connect directly to unmet needs from our early years—patterns we can observe both within ourselves and in others around us.

There is profound freedom in being able to identify which specific childhood stage our current challenges stem from.

We can invite meaning and understanding that will gently reveal the open doorway to *your* unique process and guide you back toward a sense of wholeness that belongs to you.

The truth is that unmet expectations and lingering longings are not a measure of our value, nor are they reflections of the other person's worth.

These aching longings of our childhood bring us a hidden gift:

Longings are not our weakness but a powerful call for our souls to return to the wholeness that we once knew.

"All your past, except its beauty, is gone and nothing is left but a blessing."
~ Helen Schucman, *A Course in Miracles*

The greatest mysteries of our childhood experiences become, on the one hand, our stumbling blocks, and on the other hand, the possibility to become our greatest gifts.

We will transform the buried wounds into beautiful gateways that expand to show the clear path, opening and connecting our hearts.

This journey is about remembering our origin and our shared humanity—recognizing that beneath our protective masks, we are all seeking the same thing: to connect to unconditional love within and to share that with others.

Love always lives within us. It is a beautiful dance to sense loving presence within and to observe it reflected in the other.

How is it that presence and connection are so intimately linked?

For this is the nature of our human lives, the freedom to choose each time to come back to presence within, to uplevel our deep knowing each time, to reconnect to wisdom, and to relearn each time how to love.

"The violation of the natural weakness and simplicity of the young child—these wounds may be redeemed through the natural simplicity of loving; indeed, they may offer the gateway through which love may enter."

~ Jean Houston, *The Possible Human*

We will find the ways to open our eyes and hearts to heal, to see more, with compassionate understanding, with the gift of innocent curiosity.

When we dare to feel the pain of separation rather than fight it or flee from it, something miraculous is invited in.

If you deeply desire more understanding, more fulfilling connection, we will find it, together. This is why we are here.

THE SANCTUARY OF STILLNESS

Between our longing for connection and our capacity for open, innocent perception lies a sacred threshold—a moment where we can rest before continuing our journey. This sanctuary of stillness is always available to us; it has only been forgotten in our busy lives.

In times of disconnection or confusion, we can return to this centre, to the heart, to the breath. From this place of centred awareness, we become ready to see with new eyes and perceive with the innocence that allows wonder to return to our lives.

The meditation below is an invitation to experience this sanctuary directly. Scan the QR code to listen whenever you need to reconnect with your innate stillness—particularly before exploring new perspectives or when feeling overwhelmed by the complexities of thoughts in the mind.

THE SANCTUARY OF STILLNESS MEDITATION

It is now time to begin from a place of freshness, and to explore the art of seeing with innocent eyes. This new place of seeing is the starting point of our adventure.

With renewed wonder, every encounter with another person can become an opportunity to witness a sacred being, to see the other as though for the first time, and we will come to understand that they are really part of us. "There are no strangers in God's creation" (Schucman, *A Course in Miracles*).

CHAPTER 3

INNOCENT PERCEPTION, A PLACE OF WONDER

"To see a world in a grain of sand
And Heaven in a Wild Flower
Hold Infinity on the Palm of your Hand
And Eternity in an hour"

~ **William Blake, "Auguries of Innocence"**

Young children look at the world with awe and an innate deep sense of oneness, which keeps them fully in the moment. Without the veil of preconceived thoughts or judgements, they absorb the essence of everyone and everything around them just as they are: pure and unfiltered.

So, now as adults, as we feel distracted and disconnected, how do we become more aware, more present, and stop seeing the world from our distorted viewpoint?

As we begin, we will reconnect to the tender space of childhood that many of us have closed off to or forgotten. We will open our eyes to bring in the liberating joy of seeing things differently and to ignite new opportunities.

When we set our own limiting thoughts aside, when we choose to put heaviness down to rest, we can observe the true nature of the world directly. To truly "see others," what does this mean?

Wonder, awe, and curiosity now become our guides as we revisit the journey of childhood with its deep needs and longings.

When we choose to soften and open ourselves to new perspectives, something miraculous happens. This openness creates space within us to receive deeper understanding and truly experience the essence of the people and experiences that enter our lives.

The shift in perspective—this willingness to change our opinions—brings a sense of liberation, lightness, and expansion. As multiple viewpoints become available to us, we discover newfound freedom and possibility that awakens us to life's fullness.

Valarie Kaur's work on Revolutionary Love beautifully illustrates how wonder can heal the pain of disconnection and hatred. Children naturally possess an abundance of wonder, which allows them to absorb the world around them with remarkable openness. This quality enables their incredible pace of learning and continuous growth in awareness. When we approach learning with wonder and curiosity, the struggle disappears—we remain open, vulnerably receptive yet ready, absorbing new ideas with natural ease.

To approach another person with curiosity is to truly open ourselves to them. Wonder helps us recognize the divine essence reflected in each living being. It invites us into a space of unknowing that is free from fear. Wonder grows from a place of humility—a powerful, new kind of humility—that nurtures deep reverence for life. This quality forms the foundation of true wisdom.

"May you experience each day as a sacred gift woven around the heart of wonder."

~ John O'Donohue, "For Presence"

There's no pressure to change or adopt new views. To simply wonder is a gift that keeps us close to our true nature.

Let us now take an example of a childhood memory and see how it can be transformed through a fresh perspective, while still honouring the experience of the journey.

A childhood memory that might appear trivial to an outside observer can actually hold deep significance. Beneath the surface of these seemingly small moments lie intense feelings that may have formed blocks—obstacles that prevent the full expression of self in adulthood.

These blocks limit our freedom in significant ways. While a single incident might not leave a lasting impression, repeated experiences of shame can lead the mind to develop strong, protective strategies. These strategies are triggered each time similar circumstances arise, growing stronger with each activation, even when there is no actual threat to survival.

For a developing child, the sudden shift from belonging to exclusion (without support) can be profound. Our primal brain creates warning systems around these memories, narrowing our focus from exploration to avoidance, preventing us from seeing life's full possibilities. Instead of preserving childhood wonder, these abrupt moments of disconnection become defining experiences.

SLOW

Observe carefully,
Pay attention
Assess the situation . . .
Do you see me?
Please see me!
Protect me, you are all I have.
Hold in the tears,
Must not embarrass anyone.
Be good,
Just be good.
We were playing in the driveways of each other's houses,
Neighbours and children
A hierarchy of ages with followers and leaders

All eager to belong
All looking to shine in the eyes of the Revered Ones.
I am one of the younger ones.
Then come the words:
"Not you!
Not in my team. You are too slow!"
Eyes look away,
Pretending not to care, the soft body feeling shock
Lasting out the game with great reserves:
Don't show weakness.
Then finally making it home,
Home across the road to Mother
Finally letting it out and expressing,
Expectantly reaching out:
"They said I was too slow!"
Tears hiding behind expectant and earnest eyes,
Swallowing a lump.
Then comes a short laugh, a wry smile,
Distracted, exhausted eyes of the Mother:
"Don't be so sensitive . . .
She's so sensitive, you know . . ."
From an unknowing missed opportunity,
and a programmed conditioning
Already locked in, passed on through the generations,
There is a reaction and a quick "necessary lesson."
Belief: to survive, we must toughen up; the world is harsh.
*"They are right; you **are** slow!"*
Unconscious, automatic,

Learned from the echoes of the past.
And in that,
A jolt of surprise
For the child, in the now,
A fast beating heart,
And the label is sewn onto the tags of her back,
"I am Slow."
A subtle dimming of the light,
One sparkle lost in the eye,
A formation of a link in a metal chain
As "Slow" is to be mocked—
And we can unwittingly joke about it, laugh at it,
But the joke enters a deep space of shame:
Slow is not good enough,
Slow is not belonging
And underneath that,
I am a hindrance to the game.
"Don't be so sensitive; it's not right."
I must stay alive.
Act, do not forget.
Who shall I become now
so I can be on the Team?
So I can join in the Game?

Can we connect to the feelings of that little child? We may initially think the child is too demanding, perhaps too soft. We quickly form an opinion, a conclusion. Yet, when we direct our attention gently toward the child, to imagine and to live into the story as has been described, we may start to open up to see more of the child's own experience, and our own programmed evaluations or projections may begin to move and shift.

We may now see a child who is searching for protection and the reassurance of connection, where feelings can be safely expressed, perhaps looking for the anchor point, the one who rebalances and shows how we can soothe our nervous system.

Let us take some time to explore how we might hold this childhood memory and bring it into a more conscious awareness. We can walk together to imagine the ways that can bring a sense of relief, a feeling of restoration and a return to inner freedom.

When we revisit a childhood memory we can begin to recall the voice, the gestures, the energy of our primary caregiver: the one who kept us physically alive, the one who formed the foundation of our safety and sense of security in the world.

In children under age 7, messages received at this time are taken into the body. We believe that the labels we were given are the truth.

"You are slow!"

It might seem like just a small thing, irrelevant, a casual remark. But those words—the labels—however casual they seem, become stuck in the protective layers of the subconscious. They travel through the nervous system, lodge in the organs, and slowly transform into the narrative that begins to tell the story of who we are.

This story can be likened to many other incidents, to similar labels that we received: clumsy, stupid, foolish, useless, waste of space, time-waster, daydreamer . . . the labels are endless. Even to continually label a child as a "good girl" or "clever boy" becomes a limiting view, especially as it comes with conditions of compliance.

From a childhood memory such as this, I could find that I have adopted a fixed view of myself, and I could easily resort to blaming others, carrying the belief that deep down, I wasn't as good as they were, or that I needed to live *up* to my label to be acceptable. As children, we must make sense of the world around us. To stay acceptable, to be loved, we find ways to survive.

Here is one tactic the child in this story could adopt as they adapt to fit into life:

"Don't show weakness or you'll be mocked. To be mocked means exclusion. Exclusion means you will not survive. Hide your weakness, cover up so you will not die."

This becomes another unconscious trigger, a learned response to avoid danger. "Don't show hurt feelings," and the pattern forms: withdrawal from others, like a snail retreating into its shell, whenever slowness—or any other label we were given—rears its ugly head.

Stuck in the belief that "slow" means "unworthy," deadlines could become terrifying. The locked-in programming would send signals: "You are slow, so don't even try. Freeze, and maybe no one will notice you."

This is a story containing feelings of betrayal, shock, and disconnection, the sudden rejection from the group.

And the other children? Those in the group? They were not yet aware, without guidance or a role model to show another way to care for each other; they were children still learning and experimenting.

Pain can be caused when there is a lack of understanding of the impact of actions or words. Children model everything they see and hear, without discernment. They perpetuate through the energy of unfiltered imitation of those in their environment; unkind actions are also reflections of experiences, reactions, and observed behaviours of others in their lives.

What did the hurt one need at that moment? We may have different ideas.

Connection first. Perhaps some gentle words to acknowledge the hurt, a touch—or some physical action of caring: creating a wider perspective comes after a return to safety. It is so hard to see more from a place of contraction and self-preservation.

Let us expand it now and shift our perspective.

You see what you believe. When you change your mind, the world changes.

A shift in perspective is like healing medicine.

Grounded in the body, we can now feel into our imagination—the part of our mind where ideas are not analysed but played with—and we have the power to transform old beliefs into new possibilities.

"What if"—the two magical words that we loved to use as a curious child as we dreamt up ideas for creative play—brings a new excitement and open space. The "what if" brings us to now, this moment of something not yet known. In the space of this moment, we are free from the constraint of all past thoughts—what we think is known—that which is coloured by experience.

May I welcome in an intention to see things differently . . .

REVISITING AND HEALING A CHILDHOOD MEMORY

Let's journey together to revisit and transform a story from your past. I invite you to recall a time in your childhood when you experienced disconnection or rejection.

Step 1: Create a Safe Space

Find a quiet, comfortable place where you won't be disturbed. Take a few moments to simply breathe and settle. Notice how your breath naturally flows in and out without effort. Allow your body to feel supported.

Step 2: Open to Wonder

When you feel ready, speak these words softly to yourself:

I open myself to wonder and allow this experience to speak to me now.

Step 3: Approach with Gentleness

With compassion and tenderness, allow yourself to step into the memory. There's no rush—move at your own pace. You are not reliving the pain but witnessing it with new eyes.

Step 4: Feel Without judgement

As emotions arise, simply notice them without trying to change or judge them. They are messengers carrying wisdom that only want to bring you back to your true self.

- What was I longing for at that moment?
- What did I truly need but couldn't express?
- What felt missing or lost?

Step 5: Speak to Your Inner Child

Now, as your adult self, address the child within you:

I am here now. How can I help you, dear little one? What do you need right now?

Then be still and listen. Let that younger part of you respond in whatever way feels natural—through words, images, sensations, or emotions. Create space for whatever arises.

Step 6: Discover New Possibilities

In this quiet exchange between your adult and child selves, notice what begins to emerge:

- What new understanding is forming?
- What different perspective might transform this story?
- What healing words are waiting to be spoken?

This exploration opens a doorway to new possibilities—born from wonder, vulnerability, and trust in your own inner wisdom.

Step 7: Offer Healing Words

Now, find the words that would have mattered most—words that reflect the unconditional love and acceptance your child self needed to hear. These are not words of denial but of compassionate truth.

I hear the echoes of my past pain and instead of rejecting them, I hold them gently. From this tender holding, I can find new words to give now what was needed then.

Here is my example of healing words that I found for the child who was labelled "slow":

Yes, my love, sometimes we move slowly. We can also move fast!
I am here, I see you.

You are safe. You can be slow today; slow is not wrong.
Dearest love,
Slow and thoughtful today are your gifts.
There are times for being slow, and slowness can be needed.
You can move slow AND you can move fast,
For you are all possibilities, just because you are.
Tell yourself these words:
"I exist now in this moment; I am here right now.
Now, I feel into slowness.
I take time to choose the right move;
When I slow down, I can hear what is important.
I can choose with consciousness.
I am worthy because I am."

EMBRACING NEW MEANING

I can now explore all the possibilities that may exist within this little child labelled as "slow." Now I am the adult and I can hear thoughts arise from my new way of looking

Here is my new perspective: I am curious to see what is changing within.

What if to be slow is to be tuned to intuition, to be the great observer?

This could become a great gift for the future.

Here, there is nothing to be ashamed of.

There is now a "slow movement." There is even a book about "slow."

Slow is the antidote to a frantic world. Slow is mindfulness; it is reconnection. Slow and steady wins the race. When I slow down, I open the possibility to get into flow and be attuned, to resonate and to receive the messages of what needs to be done.

There is a time for going slow and a time for speeding up. There is a time for everything.

What is done in this time, when I bring myself here and now, is what needs to be done, nothing more, on a wonderful journey of becoming and discovery.

For the old label can now become the new gift and insight.

When the old story in our mind becomes more quiet, when we realise there can be a new story created from the old, the old can be gently put aside to rest and be thanked and blessed for leading us to this new way of seeing, this expanded place of acceptance and compassion.

And then, in this new open space, in the presence we reclaimed, we can come home—home to what is—with a perception that is fresh where we are, here and now. Now we can practice this innocent perception when we want to improve our relationships, when another person brings us a challenge. With a return to presence, we ask to see afresh. We open to reveal lessons for ourselves that we did not see before, now in the reflection of the struggles of another.

"To encounter a thing as it is, without the imposition of concepts, narratives, or labels, is to grasp its essence. But how does one strip away the layers of conditioning, of learned recognition, of linguistic reference? How does perception move from structure to the formless presence of reality?"

~Siri Perera, "The Essence of Direct Experience: Seeing beyond Form"

SUPPORTING OTHERS

Drawing from a beautiful observation practice in Steiner education—also called a "Child Study" that teachers work on together—I would love to share here the suggested steps that help us connect to the compassion we have within, just waiting to be activated.

The process is a way toward healing disconnection and loving the other with humility, allowing them to become reconnected to the pure essence of themselves. This can be for our children and all our own interpersonal adult relationships.

To observe in this way is a practice that brings us closer in our hearts to another person. What we find is that when we choose to hold someone in a loving observation, in willingness for our open perception, something inside us also shifts. It involves an open and non-judgemental view, aiming to connect with the true essence of another in the most mindful and unobtrusive way. It is a *seeing* of the other with new eyes and a *listening* with the heart.

The other does not know, leaving them free to continue just as they are. There are no conditions for them; you are only holding them in your awareness. You are observing normal daily life in the moments you choose to observe in this way. Don't share your thoughts or notes with the other. This is only for your own inner processing. These are the steps:

1. **Come into deep presence within yourself** and then ask for warm interest and non-judgement. Choose a calm, quiet space and simply become aware of your breathing. Observe how your breath comes and goes without your conscious effort. Pause and be. Approach the "study" free of any preconceived notions.

2. **Prepare inwardly, setting an intention.** "I am willing to see all that is there to see. I am ready to be open and curious."

3. **Recognize the spiritual journey.** This is for both yourself and the child or adult you are observing. Remember, and have faith for the sacred core of their being.

4. **Describe carefully to yourself what you see.** First, stay as close as possible to the reality of what you *actually* see. Make notes, if you wish. Observe all the details of the person without interpretation. You may, for example, choose to describe physical attributes, or the way the other moves, eats, speaks, what their likes and dislikes are, a certain habit, and so on. Notice if you start to judge, and gently put the judgement aside. Feelings may arise in you; be aware the feelings are arising and, just for now, allow them to rest until later.

5. **Pause and become fully present again**. As you have formed the factual observation, you may now allow feelings to arise for you. As you have already made your clear descriptions, acknowledge the feelings and recognize they are yours.

6. **Ask yourself,** *where do the feelings come from?* *Are they connected to my own likes, dislikes, agreements, beliefs, or opinions?* Ask yourself if these feelings indicate the way to a new insight for the other person, and ask to understand what you are learning about yourself. There is no pressure to force anything. Only acknowledge what you notice arising within yourself.

7. **Take time.** Observe over a period of a few weeks, if possible, not just one day or one instance, so that the picture of the other begins to live in you. Take your time with the process.

8. **Use your senses to deepen your perception** (we will look at the senses more deeply in Chapter 4). Examples can be: what touches you, what do you see or hear, how does the other use speech, how do they express themselves? Bring your full attention. How do they move and interact, how do they walk, what gestures do they use? Keep reconnecting to what you feel in your body. Where do you feel it? How are you moved by your feelings?

9. **Take your reflections into sleep overnight**, asking for guidance and inspiration to bring you clear images of who this person really is. Ask a) what you might do that may help or b) if indeed anything *needs* to be done. The answer may come in the form of words, an image, or a new idea.

10. As a last step, and over time, **notice if there is any change** in yourself, in the other, or in you both, as you have held them inwardly in your loving attention.

Sometimes, we may notice a change even before we finish the process. I have seen children and adults heal, relax, and restore their own sense of joy and being. They may have a new lightness in themselves—and this is only after step 1 or 2!

I believe it is because, in our open seeing and holding of another in our seeking for their truth, we bring in a powerful healing energy that frees them, that allows them to be more of who they really are. Perhaps in holding a person in this way we can allow a hindrance that was present in them, perhaps reflected in us, to move away. It is no longer needed as we begin to resonate with their true essence, and we restore ease and natural being for us both.

When we are frustrated with someone or we feel someone is struggling with a difficulty, this process—a form of deep listening without verbal direction—shifts the focus from an inward, self-protective gesture to an outward expansion, from frustration or confusion to allowing us to engage more fully with the world and others. It marks the first step back to a restoration of our true nature, and moves us to feeling a sense of softening and expanding, bringing valuable insights and understanding for both ourselves and others.

It takes practice. We may fail. Old frustrations resurface. And we keep remembering to drop all judgement, to return to our inner place of presence. We let go of the other needing to change. We open ourselves up.

I have practiced this observation for children many times over the years. I have been astonished and moved; it feels as though a child has been blessed by a compassion that I receive from beyond my analytical mind, an unconditional love that moves way beyond the limitations of concepts. This practice has also transformed my reactions into more attuned responses with deeper understanding and compassion in the relationships in my life.

The same qualities of wonder and openness that allow us to perceive the world afresh are the very gifts that enable us to understand our earliest experiences in childhood. It is here that our story of human connection truly begins.

With the innocent perception of a young child, give yourself permission to see new possibilities. Can you now do this for yourself, for your own inner child that calls for presence and your attention?

As you use this book to reflect and process, take all the time you need; remember, the practices are yours to use at your own pace. There is nowhere you need to get to. All of who you are right now is exactly right for this moment.

"Nothing you become will disappoint me; I have no preconception that I'd like to see you be or do. I have no desire to foresee you, only to discover you. You can't disappoint me."

~Mary Haskell, *Beloved Prophet: The Love Letters of Kahlil Gibran and Mary Haskell*

Now we are ready to explore distinct stages of childhood, each step offering an opportunity to restore your sense of wholeness and ease. You may resonate with one particular stage more than another. You may wish to understand your own children better. You may be drawn to an insight into your own childhood.

This is a journey that can be done in gentleness. I remind you, once again, that this book is not intended as an instruction manual but as an invitation to be held, to receive, to explore as you rediscover more ease to be who you are, to live your life as you came here to do.

CHAPTER 4

CHILDHOOD REVISITED AND THE LEARNING JOURNEY

"Thus, again and again there recurs the miracle of man's growth, but we are so used to it that it does not arrest us as it should. The growing forces in the child are a 'living witness to God.'"

~ Caroline von Heydebrand, *Childhood: A Study of the Growing Child*

I sit at my desk, waiting for the words, asking and wondering: *What would you have me write?*

I connect to my heart. I feel very earnest, and I have a sense of surrender.

Then, I have a beautiful and powerful vision: I am tingling; a child is standing right before me, with eyes so bright, sparkling, looking clearly into my eyes. I feel astonished. The child is so full of promise. The sacred innocence in the being of the child is speaking of love.

"Have you lost your way?"
The child stretches out a hand . . . a hand to hold mine.
"Come with me once again on a journey.
I will tell you all as it is, and the forgotten truth of who you
really are will be found—
the truths of your connection to every being on this planet—
and once again, you will discover the wonder of being alive, as
you once felt,
from a time in your childhood,
for the child that lives in you now."

As I write this, I am once again tingling with the memory. I feel it again: there is a way back to true connection. It is natural; it is present and available to every single one of us!

Have you ever felt a sense of awe in the purity and lively curiosity of a child at play? Have you allowed yourself to slow down to listen to the truth of their simple, innocent words?

When we allow ourselves to soften our hearts and move into childhood being—away from our automatic programmed reaction—we begin to reconnect to an ancient wisdom.

We can be moved by the vulnerable yet clear perception of childhood, where truths are explored in the language of the soul, expressed so beautifully in movement, touch, gesture, and all the stages of creative play and learning.

The trust and delight in life that we experience in the being of a child awakens something in us long ago forgotten. The openly expressed play of the child reveals the delicate buds of gifts in growing conscious awareness.

The child's pure trust ignites in us a compassion and a new kind of wonder. If we care to watch and wonder as the child in play freely expresses all the experiences in their life from moment to moment, we then see that in each moment lies the future destiny of a growing human being where all things are becoming possible.

For in the process of living is life itself; our life is happening in every moment and not waiting until we reach a perfection point. In the present moment, the answers to our questions are waiting. The solutions to our problems may unfold; and our perceived destination may change as we begin to listen.

We felt this once, in our bodies and our hearts; our innate bodily intelligence opened us to the next stage, the flow of imagination, to create with the things of the world, and then play with the ideas. This is the true meaning of creative play. Our childlike hopefulness in each new day may have become hidden in the striving of our adult lives. Perhaps we forgot about our real play—our doorway to creation—yet imaginative play is the gift that never leaves us.

See how to make every day a new place to begin again, to move into an uplifted and expanded place. We will follow the child—the child in us—walking again with curiosity for truth.

The greatest importance is to take care not to block that true knowing voice inside of you. It can easily be shut down by the critical voice in your head and the one outside that judges and shames.

It is the knowing voice—not from a fragmented part of you and not from the coldness of intellect alone, not from the array of thoughts that come and go, but from the still essence of your being—that is whole and complete. It is this voice that waits within you as your wisdom *just for you* to access your truth, to hear what is the action for you that you will feel called to take.

So let your inner wisdom be heard and become your guide.

There will be no fixed formula, no mandatory prescriptions, no manipulation or distraction from our truth. We will ignite new possibilities. We will enter with our imagination and explore together. We will restore the sense of who we are, understanding with compassion the lingering longings and needs and meet them now. We will learn to see with new eyes and open our hearts with a soft curiosity.

Let us take a moment and pause.

I invite you to sit with the meditation below to enter the open space of wonder—like that of the child—to reconnect with the space of your heart and be ready to contemplate our learning journey, not as an exercise of concepts but as a world of discovery.

Meditation *(Inspired by John O'Donohue's "For Presence" and the wisdom of childhood wonder.)*

Find a comfortable position. Allow your body to settle.

Take a deep cleansing breath in, and a long, slow breath out.

Become aware now of your breathing, as your chest and your lower belly expand and contract. Allow it to find its rhythm, soft and natural.

Relax into this gentle space.

Imagine yourself as a child at the threshold of discovery.

Your eyes are wide and clear, unclouded by judgement or expectation.

The world is not yet divided into categories.

Everything is possibility. Everything is wonder.

Breathe in the innocence of pure perception.

Listen to these words from the poem, "For Presence":

> *When you slip beneath the surface of things,*
> *Beyond the familiar landscape of your thoughts,*
> *A different source of knowing begins to stir*

Feel the invitation to see beyond what you think you know, to release the tight grip of your adult perceptions, to return to a state of open curiosity.

Your body remembers this state of wonder—before analysis, before criticism—when each moment was a revelation.

Breathe into the space of not knowing.

Feel the gentle awakening of your senses:

- the touch of air on your skin,

- the subtle sounds around you,
- the play of light behind your closed eyes,
- the rhythm of your breath.

No need to understand. Simply be present.

Whisper to yourself:

"I allow myself to see with new eyes. I welcome wonder. I am open to the mystery."

Imagine a child's hand reaching out to touch the world: curious, unafraid, sensing everything as if for the first time.

Beneath the surface of things, a different knowing emerges

Soft as breath, vast as silence, gentle as a child's wonder.

Feel how your perception begins to shift, how judgement softens, how curiosity awakens.

You are remembering something ancient, a way of seeing that is pure, unfiltered, alive with possibility.

Take a deep breath. Feel the child within you stirring: eager, loving, whole.

Rest here quietly for a minute, nowhere to be, nothing to do.

When you are ready, gently open your eyes.

Let the things you see around now be seen with your fresh eyes.

See the world as if for the first time.

In this moment, you are both the observer and the observed.

Carry this sense of wonder with you.

Every moment is an invitation

To wonder, to see, to just be.

Here we are now. Come with me. We have arrived at the next step. The scene is set. We are ready to explore the miracle of human learning in all its wonder.

THE LEARNING JOURNEY: A SPIRAL OF BECOMING

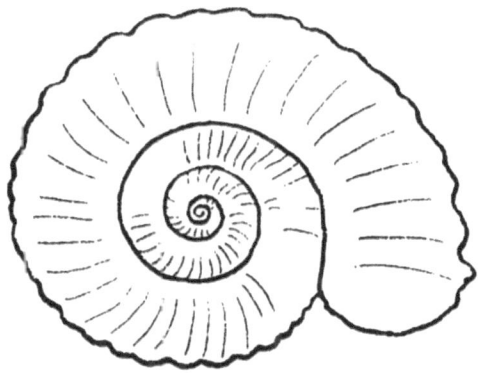

Have you ever watched a baby discovering their hands or feet? In the adult who pauses to notice, and in the full absorption of the baby, something ignites: pure awe and joy in witnessing this moment of total focussed attention.

Our learning in life follows a mysterious path. We don't always understand the lessons immediately. Our journey mirrors a spiral—an ever-widening path of growth where each turn honours the past whilst reaching for boundless potential. It unfolds in distinct stages, dancing between certainty and wonder.

What if learning is less about acquiring and more about allowing, about creating room for something to breathe, to unfold in its own time? I've watched children learn—not the structured learning of classrooms but the wild, unpredictable exploration that happens in moments of pure wonder. As we move through life, we can choose to hold on to that curiosity, creating spaces where learning isn't forced or hurried but moves as freely as breath.

When learning flows naturally—from the instinctual responses of the newborn to the inspired creations of the adult—we experience fulfillment, purpose, and a return to our natural state. For children, what cements learning is the glue of trusting relationships. Only when rooted in essential connection can a child's natural curiosity fully blossom, propelling them outward to discover their world with genuine wonder.

All learning is given wings when we have someone to accompany us, help us digest new skills, and share in the magic of our becoming.

Sometimes, lost in what feels like struggle, we forget the miracle of how we learn. The whispers of inspiration fade beneath life's noise. But the child remembers.

Watch a child unfold into being, and you witness the path we all travel.

First comes instinct—those seeds already planted in our garden. The body knows without being told, formed from invisible, powerful wisdom, an energy beyond thought or control. A newborn turns toward warmth, cries for nourishment. These primal rhythms prepare the vessel, creating beneath our feet the ground from which everything grows.

Then imitation blooms. With no filter between self and world, the child becomes a perfect mirror. Every cell vibrates in attunement with those they love. They don't simply copy; they are devoted, drawn unconsciously to the mysterious essence of spirit. They absorb the world with their entire being, not through conscious choice but through pure resonance, the beginning of all connection.

Imagination arrives like a beam of light as inner pictures form, and speech and memory awaken. The child who once only imitated now creates. Their body becomes an instrument playing its own songs. In play, children dream: reality feels fixed, but imagination is boundless. Through it, wooden blocks transform into wondrous palaces. Cardboard boxes, coloured cloths, and garden sticks become magnificent ships sailing across imagined seas.

Innovation emerges as imagination takes flight, taking what was given and reshaping it into what has never been. Something flashes through our experiments: a new idea, a fresh connection. We remix and create, offering unique expression to the world.

Inspiration finds its voice when what began in the body expands beyond the individual, touching something larger than ourselves. We open beyond the limited thinking mind to receive wisdom that seems to flow from the universe itself.

This spiral never ends. Whenever we approach life with childlike openness, we dance through this sequence again in all new learning—a perpetual source of joy, a chance to play.

SURRENDERING AND LETTING GO OF OLD LEARNING

From the body's wisdom, through devoted mirroring into playful imagination and innovative creation, inspiration arrives as we allow and receive.

Guiding wisdom can be heard through a mind cleared of sensation and conceptual self, opening a portal to divine creation. Free of old patterns, supported by beauty in the heart, this is the point—the portal— where we release what we think we need to know, making space for something uniquely expressed to emerge. The old learning that served now transforms as the spark received deeply within.

Inspiration brings insights for the greater good. When we act from this place, connected to Divine Source, we are guided in ways that benefit everything around us. This learning journey feels like a miracle—transformation layering upon transformation, branching outward, expanding the curve, stretching into infinite possibility, always connected to Source, alive and in movement.

I once encountered a program called Watch, Wait, and Wonder that heals parent-child relationship difficulties through presence and gentle observation. I was deeply moved by parents' experiences—how they reconnected with something profound they'd forgotten in daily living. In the quiet attention of the adult, the child's needs become clear, seen from a place of awakened compassion that moves the adult deeply. Relationships strengthen, and the child's true being emerges free of adult judgement, expectations, and anxiety.

As we progress through life, we develop the ability to observe others' learning journeys with awe. By recognizing where someone struggles in a particular phase, empathy is awakened in us for their path.

When we reflect on our own journey and understand the humanness of our processes, we begin to feel compassion for ourselves and for the capacities we once saw as imperfect or incomplete.

Key Takeaways

- Childhood (age birth to 7): Defined by instinct and imitation, laying groundwork for future development as imagination gradually awakens.

- Middle years (age 7 through middle school): Imagination and creativity take flight, inviting exploration, play with ideas, and self-expression.

- Adolescence (age 14 to 21): Innovation becomes the focus as boundaries are tested, new ideas form, and sense of self develops. Inspiration appears when teens feel safe expressing themselves.

- Adulthood: Brings opportunity for reflective inspiration where experience transforms into wisdom and deeper understanding.

  - As we move between instinct, imitation, imagination/innovation, and inspiration, each new understanding reshapes our world, bringing expansion, joy, and energy.

  - Our inner wisdom serves as the compass harmonizing our human learning capacities, knowing intuitively which aspect is needed at any moment.

This quiet voice at our centre doesn't keep us fixed in any mode but helps us flow naturally between body, mind, and spirit—grounding us in instinct when needed, resonating through imitation, playing and creating in imagination, making new inventions, and surrendering to inspiration.

True wisdom emerges at the balance point where all aspects of our learning journey meet in harmony, where inspired thought becomes alive as inner knowing, strong within our centre—our sacred place that holds and allows a beautiful process to exist.

To be fully alive is to remain open to this dance, allowing our inner compass to navigate the ever-unfolding path of human discovery.

Pause. Rest. Digest. Learning new concepts is an adventure. Thoughts are only thoughts. Without stillness and rest, we might feel ourselves spiraling out instead of participating in life's dance from the solid anchor of our being. I have made a diagram that you can find in appendix 1 illustrating the journey of learning and the inner compass of wisdom at the centre.

And now, when you are ready, we will move to the next step in understanding our wonderful human experience: you are invited to explore the world of our senses.

Have you ever wondered about the gifts of your senses—how beautifully designed we are as sensory beings?

What I have come to see is that our senses create an exquisite bridge between our inner world and everything we encounter outside. Like delicate, perfectly calibrated instruments, senses help us navigate the boundaries between self and other—between what is me and what is not me.

They are sacred gateways where connection begins—with ourselves, others, and nature. They are gifts created for our human experience, allowing us to move between quiet stillness and deep attention, to dance between us as we touch the hearts of each other and the living world.

CHAPTER 5

THE TWELVE SENSES AS GATEWAYS

"We can see time and again that all of our senses are great teachers of man if only he will open his spiritual ear to this."

~Albert Soesman, *Our Twelve Senses: How Healthy Senses Refresh the Soul*

We are all gifted with senses. Could you consider the possibility that we have twelve?!

Rudolf Steiner and others after him have described twelve senses in great detail. Senses shape our human experience as spiritual beings living within physical forms. As gateways from our body to the outside, they open and interact in their own time, developing through childhood as ways of experiencing and connecting with our sense of self, with each other, and with the world.

Over the years, as I have worked with children and adults, I have started to feel more deeply how incredible it is that we each experience the world in our own way. Some of us feel everything so intensely, while others seem less affected by the sensory whirlwind around us. How is it that I smell everything so acutely, and you struggle to identify the effect of strong odours; you love the taste of durian fruit, and I like mushrooms; you are feeling too hot, whilst I need more clothes for warmth; you prefer the humid weather, and I like the arid? You may think a story is lighthearted, quite amusing even, and the other person listening to the same words is feeling deeply sad.

THE TWELVE GATEWAYS TO FULL EXPRESSION AND THE THREE LAYERS OF SENSING

Here I share a simple overview, highlighting my current and ever-evolving understanding from my perspective and from what I have learnt, practiced, and observed. This chapter is not a full deep dive into the study of the senses but a simple introduction with a hope that I will ignite your interest in the possibility of further exploration, if you are called to do so.

Let us now explore how each phase of childhood emphasises a different set of senses.

Bodily senses (Limbs, Skin, Bones): Touch, Life, Movement, Balance (0–7 years)

Middle senses (Organs and Circulation): Warmth, Taste, Smell, Sight (7–14 years)

Higher senses (Mind, Ears, and Neural Networks connected to all parts of our being, moving through the Heart): Hearing, Speaking, Thinking, Sense of the Other (14–21 years)

Let us find an imaginative way to wonder about our twelve senses to help open up to receiving, exploring, and developing your own images within—images that will help you understand just what you need in your unique way. When we bring attention to our senses, we find they will lead us back to greater presence. This is a pathway to access and exchange deeper wisdom and insights to live a full life.

OUR SENSORY DEVELOPMENT: A NATURAL UNFOLDING

To understand how these twelve senses develop, let's visualize the process through the image of a growing plant.

The senses unfold in us throughout our lives, like the seed sprouting and then growing into a plant. Describing the maturing of the senses in this way illustrates how we are designed to unfold in our own time and in our own way.

In the three foldness of our being—body, heart (soul), and mind/spirit—we grow physically upward, orienting ourselves toward the light of our higher senses with increasing self-awareness.

The roots in a plant are invisible, becoming strong in the warmth of the nurturing soil, just as the foundational learning of a young child strengthened in the warmth of relationship seems to be deep within and invisible to the human eye. In our body, the foundational senses of touch, life, movement, and balance give us our grounding and keep us stable.

Like the channeling stem, moving the sap to the sprouting leaves of a plant, our senses develop alongside the rhythmic movements of fluids within our bodies—the circulation of our blood—the flow of emotions, and the air we breathe. These exchanges, at the core of our being, vital and rhythmic, sustain us and allow us to flourish.

We strengthen our core in the heart during the middle stage of childhood, feeling called to the beauty of the world, delighting in warmth, taste, smell, and sight and a developing interest in the being of the other. The exchanges of water and gases through the leaves echo the exchanges and connections we build with our environment and the people we meet.

As we mature, through the ability of the thinking mind, we blossom into full expression. As fully realized adults, we bear fruit and flowers as we experience a sense of our uniqueness and at the same time follow our natural pull to connect with others.

As mature adults, when we are open to the light of our being, we can realise our gifts and go on to produce the seeds for the future.

All the senses flow together and form part of the whole. Each sense adds to the others, expanding and enriching our experiences. They are like lights on the path to full realization. They are joyful healers, nurturing us as we grow, creating new seed pods—like our deeds on Earth—that leave lasting impressions. Released in service, these impressions are planted for the future to multiply and to give new life.

The pace at which this process unfolds, along with the interaction of our environment and early relationships, determines the unique expression of our being within the body.

BODILY SENSES AND THE FOUNDATION OF OUR BEING

Just as the roots are vital to a plant's development, our foundational bodily senses create the necessary grounding for all that follows.

As we begin our earthly journey, we have imagined being planted on earth, our body establishing its roots, grounding us into physical existence. We can imagine growing roots deeply and invisibly underground. Like a child in the first seven years of life, the roots are vital to the health and future vitality of the whole plant.

Relationships in the early years are built from the basic caregiving we receive, and the gestures and respectful tender—or not so tender—nature of this care go deeply into our very being. Whatever is taken in—

the love we receive—shapes us in all ways and becomes absorbed into our physical body.

Touch—the first experience of the boundary between self and world, between what is me and what is sensed as the other;

Life—the sense of well-being in the body, linked to the sensations of ease or discomfort;

Self-Movement—our experience of motion in space, which relates to our biographical path and autonomy;

Balance—our orientation in space, closely tied to movement, the workings of the inner ear, stillness, and our ability to listen.

Our unfolding and expression are perfect and unique to our individual journey; as the senses interact and merge with each other, so do our capacities of body, heart, and mind become integrated. The pace at which this happens—whether forced, fertilised, protected, or neglected, determines the unique expression of our emerging being.

All of us would feel blessed to awaken at our own pace; we hope we meet the right conditions, the supportive parents and teachers, to allow the time that is required for our unique full potential to blossom. Yet all will unfold exactly as it needs to. However the emerging of our soul appears, it is always perfectly timed.

The rose is a rose
from the time it is a seed
to the time it dies.
Within it, at all times,
it contains its whole potential.

It seems to be constantly
in the process of change;

Yet at each state, at each moment,
it is perfectly all right as it is.

~Tim Gallwey, *The Inner Game of Tennis*

SENSING IN TODAY'S WORLD AND SENSES AS HEALING

While the senses are naturally designed to help us navigate our world, the modern environment presents unique challenges to their healthy functioning.

In today's fast-paced, overstimulated world, most of us struggle with the amount of sensory input available. Some things we can shut out, and many times we have learnt that survival means numbing ourselves.

It feels so hard to come to a sense of clarity when we are pulled in so many different directions, often hooked deliberately. So much of our time is spent living in a reactive state, not realizing the extent to which we are being manipulated and prevented from hearing the voice of wisdom—the wisdom that is needed in our own situations for the people we love and for our own unique sense of agency and purpose.

This is what we learn as the world becomes louder, more competitive, apparently more false. We worship the intellect but feel a gaping hole in our innermost being. We are far too afraid to surrender to a place of not knowing, of acknowledging feelings and sensing truth in our bodies.

Our feelings are held within the physiology of our bodies: the tissues, the lungs, the stomach, the heart. These emotions are intimately linked to our sense of life—visible in the quickening or slowing of circulation, the churning of digestion, the warming or cooling of blood flow. When we feel passion or fear, our blood flows faster, our heart beats louder and quicker. We might feel sick in our stomach with a sense of dread, our muscular tissue seizing up with prolonged tension and anxiety, our breathing constricted in anticipation or fear.

Through movement, we express what words can't—a hand clenched in anxiety, shoulders curled inward in protection. Even how we interpret what we see becomes coloured by the emotions flowing through us, transforming situations into perceived threat or comfort.

How would it feel to learn to listen again to the communications within the body, to be able to hear the messages, to allow the flow, to create more space for ourselves and others?

The loss of the sense of self may have been experienced unconsciously during childhood in challenging times when the connected, supportive presence of an adult was not available or when we were not able to express ourselves through the body's ability to communicate. In sensory awareness practice, or somatic experiencing, we can begin to reconnect to the sensations in the body in the present moment, experiencing how movement and emotions communicate.

SENSORY AWARENESS PRACTICE

Recognizing these challenges, we can turn to practices that help us reconnect with our sensory wisdom.

This journey of reconnecting with our senses opens a beautiful path toward discovering our true selves. By turning our attention inward, we can begin healing those fragmented parts that developed during our childhood years. Understanding when and where each of our senses formed gives us insight into our unique developmental story. When we practice bringing mindful attention to our sensory experiences, we gradually reclaim a feeling of autonomy within our bodies, accessing more of our inherent potential.

The Sensory Awareness Foundation is one example of such a healing experience and reconnection to the body's wisdom (https://sensoryawareness.org). You can find free experiences and online classes as well as longer retreats where you can practice bringing back connection to self with compassion.

I have taken intensive sessions in sensory awareness to help with my support of parents of young children. These sessions were profoundly impactful and also improved my ability to listen to the communication being expressed by children through their bodies. I experienced a deep sense of reconnection with my body's own knowing and learnt how to create more nurturing environments that support both children and adults in resetting and restoring wellbeing. I love incorporating this practice to find more presence and groundedness.

It is a continual practice, allowing the expression of what is felt: observing and allowing the breath and the body to show us how it needs to be and move. We find we are usually pushing and trying so hard to fix ourselves. These practices feel even better when we are held within the safety and support of a loving person. It can be gentle and reverent to release the deepest stuck emotions. With these senses, which are always developing and being refined from birth, we create more open space inside ourselves for presence to what is and to connect more deeply with what needs to be heard.

This is a testimonial documented on The Sensory Awareness Foundation website:

> *Individual sessions let me explore being with and finding "here" no matter what is whirling around in my head or life. Your willingness and ability to sit and track what is arising in me, directly asking questions and honestly making suggestions, feels like the open-handed, open-hearted love I missed as a child. I like living, when I can, from this place of child-like wonder with solid ground under me. This feels like true life, true me.*

When we return to the felt language of the body—the warmth of touch, the rhythm of breath, the subtle whispers of intuition—we reunite with parts of ourselves long silenced by the noise of doing. It means embracing full presence as we inhabit each sensation fully, allowing our nervous systems to rewrite stories of disconnection. In this sensory remembering, we discover ourselves in a fresh way.

With our listening, we become freer to hear more, to listen for clarity and truth. With our speaking, we allow what needs to be spoken to flow through us. Each day that we are alive and aware, the senses open us to the miracle of being human.

There are never enough words to describe a sensory experience, and as we analyse a sense we seem to lose our ability to fully feel. The purpose of senses is to know that we can develop and fine-tune throughout our lives. These senses help us find stability when needed, creating a grounded place from which we can relate more authentically to others. This gentle practice helps heal the disconnect between our awareness now and the wisdom our bodies have always carried, creating a more whole and true way of being.

THE THREE PHASES OF SENSORY DEVELOPMENT

Returning to our developmental framework, we can now summarize how these twelve senses unfold through the three phases of childhood.

In the first seven years, the senses of touch, life, movement, and balance are all connected to our body. They are focussed within. These senses are predominant in Part One: Truth in the Body.

95

In the middle stage, from age 7–14, through sight, warmth, smell, and taste we strengthen the heart forces and life processes of circulation and breathing, developing our love of and interest in the world and the other people in it. We expand outward in learning, and we take this learning as a felt inner memory, becoming more able to express our experiences of deep feelings as well as likes and dislikes. They are moving and changing, lively and creative. These senses form part of our journey found in Part Two: Beauty in the Heart.

As we move toward full adulthood, ages 14–21, we blossom into a mature expression of our unique self using the four higher senses—the flowers and the fruits on the expanding branches—which are developing thinking skills, communication skills for both listening and speaking, and a sense for self and the other person. With these senses we wake up to the capacities of the mind, discovering a sense of what is goodness along with rational thought and moral action. We learn to connect to the intelligence of the built up forces, strengthened from truth felt in the body and warmth of love in the heart of the previous stages. These higher senses reach out to connect with and develop a deeper understanding of others. They are uniquely human. They are the focus of Part Three: Goodness in the Spirit.

THE JOURNEY TO LOVE

Beyond these twelve senses lies perhaps the most profound human capacity of all.

Ultimately, we are all here to learn to love. We could even say unconditional love is our thirteenth sense, and as human beings, it is this love that we find back in our centre, awake and in full awareness of our being.

Life becomes richer through these gateways that connect us to ourselves, our inner wisdom, and the beauty of God reflected in the world and in each other. Think of this introduction to the senses as the opening of another door to a world worth exploring. As you go about your day, you might start noticing little things—how food really tastes, the feeling of a breeze on your skin, or the comfort of a familiar voice—and find yourself feeling more alive, more present in your body.

That is the gift our senses offer us every day: a way back to feeling the miracle of being alive, right here, right now. Nothing complicated required—just a gentle shift in attention to what's already happening.

We can be full of wonder as we observe the uniqueness of our children as they enjoy and expand out into the world. This lifelong relationship with our own sensory awareness brings us renewed appreciation for the miracle of embodied existence throughout our lives.

DOORWAY TO THE PARTS

As we now move into the three separate parts of Truth, Beauty, and Goodness, this summary below of the childhood needs and subsequent longings that develop in adulthood will give us a structure of support. We can now venture into each of the three childhood stages.

Exploring each of the three phases may help you connect more deeply with your children, and at the same time connect you to the forgotten needs of your own childhood to understand how you may still have unconscious longings in your life now.

We will see how to come back to true inner freedom, to no longer feel so tightly held and bound in the limiting beliefs and painful memories of the past.

These needs have been identified as universal human needs, described in various therapies relating to inner child work. They give us a map to navigate and honour each of the three phases of childhood.

At the end of each part, I have brought the essentials together so that we can see more clearly and understand better what we might now feel is missing.

The longings we carry are lights on our path, guiding us back to our wisdom.

As we learn to meet our longings with loving awareness, we discover that what we sought outside from others—revealed by the obstacles in our relationships—was always waiting within. And at the same time, in reciprocity, as the longings are calling to us to open up, it is also in sharing with others and listening with kindness, that our own healing is naturally supported in the vulnerable space between us.

I like to imagine our inner wisdom as the stabilizing point of a compass—constant and true, waiting to point us home when we choose to allow what arises, to slow down and listen.

Security & Trust (0–7 Years): Physical Care, Safety, Closeness

In our earliest years, we need consistent nurturing to build trust. When our needs go unmet, we develop a hollow space within. The forming of an internal compass is weakened early on; as we struggle with clear direction, the needle spins anxiously. We feel a void that manifests as chronic insecurity in adulthood, making trusting others difficult while we constantly seek someone to provide the safety we missed.

Love & Warm Enthusiasm (7–14 Years): Connection, Affection, Support

During these years, genuine connection helps calibrate our inner compass through being truly seen and having our feelings validated. When love is conditional, we are constantly pulled toward others for external validation. This creates a persistent hunger for confirmation of our worthiness from outside ourselves, and we become judgemental and critical of others, reflecting the inner emptiness of our feeling life. Care and curiosity for others is strengthened by the way our parents, and those in our close circles, model open non-judgement and inclusion of others.

Inner Freedom (14–21 Years): Autonomy, Independent Thinking

In adolescence, we need space to navigate with our own compass through meaningful choices. Without this freedom, we enter adulthood with untested direction, manifesting as self-doubt and dependence on others' opinions. Our compass seems off, as though it is calibrated to someone else's true north, leaving us struggling to connect authentically to our true being and to others.

As we learn to hear and honour these longings, they become like magnets that realign our inner compass. As adults, in healing our own directional systems, we become beacons for the children in our lives— those we care for now and those parts of ourselves still waiting to be found and brought home.

I will help you create examples of words you may use to support you through a phase in your childhood journey, to bring comfort to yourself now, in gentleness, that will realign you with your essential nature.

You may then naturally come to choose your own healing words, just right for you, that nurture and remind you of your inherent worthiness. Perhaps you will write down what words come for you, using the healing process of journaling. Your words can become your powerful healers, creating ease, safety, and pointing you to the truth, igniting actions you can take for you, restoring and remembering your true self.

The companion workbook is designed to deepen your process as you move through the insights offered. Through the carefully crafted prompts and reflective questions, you will have the opportunity to reconnect with these formative stages of your life—not to linger longer than you need to in the past but to heal what needs healing, receiving the gifts from these challenges that have been waiting to be seen. It is a deeply nurturing experience to be able to walk through the workbook with actual human companions. I have created groups, Listening Sanctuaries, where I support readers who would like to enter deeper into this work.

In this way you can come into the moment, release the old, and remember that now is when everything can start again.

PART
ONE

TRUTH IN THE BODY
AGES 0–7

Within flesh and bones is a knowing
Deeper than language,
Beyond the stories we construct,
Each cell a silent witness.
The body speaks what the mind has forgotten,

A language of sensation, subtle movements, and deep impressions.
Listen to the whispers beneath your protection of skin
Where spirit meets matter in soft conversation.
The first chapter unfolds,
Traced in heartbeat,
Mapped in nerve.
A truth lies waiting.
The body remembers love
Before words could speak.

We begin Part One where human experience originates—in the form of the body. As sensory beings our earliest wisdom came through what was felt in our physical bodies.

In this section, we explore how our bodies hold the unspoken truths of our existence: the sacred imprint of our birth, the neural pathways formed through our earliest attachments, and the architecture of our physical being developed through the foundation senses. These embodied realities shape us in ways that began before conscious awareness, yet continue to influence every aspect of how we relate to ourselves and others.

By turning our attention to the wisdom held within our physical form, beneath the stories and adaptations we made, we can find the original authentic knowing: truth in the body supports the formation of that inner compass that guides us back to our natural state of connection, presence, and wholeness.

The chapters that follow invite you to reconnect with this bodily truth, not as an intellectual exercise but as a felt experience that reawakens your innate capacity to live from a place of genuine attunement to yourself, those you love, and those you have yet to meet.

CHAPTER 6

OUR PATH TO BIRTH

Our birth is but a sleep and a forgetting
The soul that rises with us, our life's Star,
Hath had elsewhere its setting.
And cometh from afar:
Not in entire forgetfulness,
And not in utter nakedness,
But trailing clouds of glory, do we come
From God, who is our home

~ William Wordsworth, *Ode: Intimations of Immortality*
from Recollections of Early Childhood

When we allow ourselves to soften our hearts as we uncover the potential we have for a greater, more open, curious seeing of childhood phases—not viewing them from our past conditioning or beliefs but simply being ready and open to find out more—we make a space within. We begin to recognise the sacredness of the mystery of who we really are. In this open space that we choose to create, we begin to reconnect to an ancient wisdom: the one we came with at birth.

Our human journey naturally begins in falling asleep to our true spiritual origin, and our purpose is to remember and recognise the truth of who we are at our core, in conscious awareness. We originated in peace and wholeness. As Wordsworth so beautifully described, we are born of a wisdom that begins life in a hazy forgetfulness, though we come fresh from the spiritual world. We see traces of this ancient wisdom in the eyes of a newborn; babies have the echo of heaven around them, which perfectly draws others in.

This chapter invites us back to our beginnings—back to our sacred origin—to remember wisdom came with us, gifted deeply as our essential being in an innate form. As babies, our instinctive and intuitive self was guided by our spiritual nature, driven from the unconscious depths.

With unconscious, deep wisdom we are guided toward our greatest power as human beings. This begins as we search for and find a reflection of ourselves in the connection to another: in seeing and being seen, in the exchange between hearts that heals all fear and sense of separation.

Our sense of self began to emerge in the soul food we received when we were seen, loved, and held in the eyes and heart of our very first encounter, our first connection with another human being, and even further back in sensing the energetic love as we were held and formed in the body from our Spiritual Mother—the Creator—under our human mother's heart.

"We are born of Love; Love is our mother."

~ Rumi

I can feel a childlike excitement rising up, and a calm mother's soothing voice, as we step onto this new path. The voice—and pure presence—is of the Divine Mother, communicating with us as we find the way back to unconditional love.

I feel a strong pull to follow the archetype of the elder and sage, and I am drawn to the wisdom of the Universal Mother. This is a nurturing energy that lives in us all, no matter our gender, that we know, deep down, loves us no matter what we do. I am filled with a desire to reconnect you to who you truly are, to provide the soothing you may be longing for, to see with new eyes the gifts from your childhood—to see childhood as a divine rite of passage, a sacred journey to bring you to the place of inner freedom that leads you back to you.

Hearts open in the nurturing energy of mothering that is both gentle and firm, strong yet soothing. It is a love that is unconditional and will be a stand for you to connect to your truth, even through any necessary pain of learning. This love knows that the learning, though painful, will lead you back to you. It is:

- a nurturing that does not overpower but empowers;

- a willingness to bear it with you, to protect you from unnecessary harm but not hinder you from the lessons you are here to learn;

- the care and attention that fills you, recognising the gaps as they become the gifts that bring you back to connection within yourself. You realise: you were never *not* whole.

We are all an expression of God, of Spirit, of Divine Source, whatever name feels good to you; we are made of unconditional love.

We are from the One, here to have a human experience. In body, heart, and mind, we are here to recognise who we are, expressed here as our spirit fills this form. Seemingly separate, yet always as apparent individuals from the One Spiritual Source, never separate from the One.

Right now, at this very moment, a miracle of new life is unfolding somewhere in the world—a child will arrive on earth. A heart beats, and with each birth a first breath is taken. It is all part of a beautiful, eternal story. The dance of creation that flows through all the generations happens in the eternal now.

Feel the air you breathe. Breathe in deeply. The in-breath connects you to when you were born—that extraordinary moment when you arrived on earth—and the out-breath to when you will return to the spirit world at death. Feel the rhythms of the in and the out, the pure presence of aliveness here in this moment on earth.

Feel the ground under you, holding you up, keeping you safe. Look around. The rocks, clouds, rivers, swaying treetops, every mineral, every plant, every creature are all the heartbeat of the world. You are part of the dance between consciousness and creative energy.

How does it feel to hold this awareness in your present experience?

I invite you to come into a deeper presence now with your own creative essence.

The Mother, the bearer of my life, is the one who welcomed me into this new world.

What if this life is perfectly designed for me here and now, just as it is: the parents, the circumstances, the challenges?

Could it be that the child and the parents knew each other long ago? What if, back in time, this meeting was already written, like a sacred contract? Is our birth experience a shared agreement made between mother and child?

What is the story—your story and mine—when spirit came into matter to experience the miracle of human life?

I remember my training with a group called BabyCalm. We explored the challenges of becoming a new mother—that overwhelming time when women often feel disconnected from their inner wisdom. Our goal was to help mothers reconnect to the wonder of new life and remember they could access their own natural wisdom to understand their babies' experiences.

And then we worked in two groups: one listing all the felt emotions of the new mother and the other the imagined experience of the new baby. This awakened a new understanding and compassion that I did not think was possible, that went beyond the advice and the textbooks, the lists of dos and don'ts. It's a true inner knowing that makes such deep sense.

Here is an imaginary letter I wrote after this training, from the baby to the mother:

Dear One,

I come to you from the cosy warmth, deeply held within. My soul knew the way, and my body found its shape inside your body. I drink sweet water here, and everything I need comes to me right away. I hear your heartbeat all around me, and strange quiet sounds from somewhere far away.

A tiny light begins to glow as gentle squeezes hug me and hands pat the soft nest where I float. Love is all I know. And now I feel you too.

In this dreamy, forever place, I hear a small voice calling. Something inside both of us says it's time. We picked each other long ago—me to be your little one and you to be my mother.

Our bodies make special magic that says, "I'm ready" and "It's time to come," like tiny love notes flowing in your blood. Will you say yes?

The journey starts, held tight and squeezed, rocking, moving, and then—so much space all around!

Air fills my chest—my first big breath. Cold washes over my skin, sounds rush in, smells find my nose, and light floods in and out of my blinking eyes.

Where are you, my special one? Whose hands are holding me? Soft and steady, quick and busy, or so tender and gentle? Your touch tells me things without words.

All my feelings mix together in my small body. Like a tiny flower, I open and close with each new feeling.

I look for your warm body to snuggle against. I find your smell that I already know. Will you gently touch my face, hold my little hands, and kiss my tiny toes? I was all wrapped up inside, and now I wave my arms in the big open air. My fingers grab and hold tight. I am a little spark living in this new body. I am Spirit in a sensing body. I do not remember.

I float in this in-between place. I hear your voice singing to me. I feel your eyes watching over me. You hold me close to your warm heart. Your soft words calm my body. My breathing matches yours again. You rock me gently, like I was rocked before.

My eyes look and find yours. In that special moment, a light jumps between us from long ago—our heart journey—I found you again. Open eyes, new heart, pure feeling. Open, innocent, instinct.

What do we see in our eyes of knowing that takes us both back before time began?

I am here. I am ready. So much to learn. So much to give.

Yours in Devotion,
X

Could it be that all the encounters, all my relationships, are already agreed upon, like reflections of God, to help me remember who I am? And I am here to do the same for you?

Because you saw me, I came into existence. The being of mother also came into existence, and a new human life arrived for a new journey.

THE SONG OF WELCOME

There is a beautiful legend about a tribe in Africa where each person has their own unique song that is created by their mother before they are born. I am deeply moved by the idea of a story or song that ignites the remembering of a sacred origin.

When a woman of the tribe discovers she is pregnant, she goes out into the wilderness and listens for the song of the child she is carrying. Once she hears the song, she returns to the tribe and teaches it to the father, then to the village's midwives, and eventually to all the members of the tribe. The song becomes the child's personal melody, a unique identity.

The song is sung when the child is born, welcoming them into the world. It is then sung during important life events: reaching milestones, becoming an adult, and getting married.

If the person ever commits a wrong or strays from the tribe's values, the community gathers in a circle around them and sings the person's song to remind them of who they truly are. What a beautiful, sacred way for souls to heal and reconnect with their essence and the community!

Yet, whilst safety lies in the embrace of the group, there are moments in our lives when courage for new discoveries and expressions of the truth may not bring everyone else along. The safety of our tribe may sometimes hold us back in times for speaking our truth, when courage is needed and change is called for.

With a new compassion fuelled by the remembering of who we are, we can learn to love better.

For those who are not yet ready to change and move toward a new future: be held in love.

For those who look to a new future and travel new roads: be held in love.

Because you exist, you are worthy . . . to be held in love.

Click the QR code to access a birthday story to help you reconnect to your own sacred origin:

Here is a poem version.

Birthday Poem

Once upon a time in the starry skies,
A star child danced with twinkling eyes.
Amidst her friends, she'd laugh and play,
Visiting the sun and moon each day . . .

Her angel guarded, pure and bright,
Guiding her with love's soft light.
One night, safe in her angel's embrace,
She glimpsed a new, enchanting place.

Down to Earth, their journey led,
Where oceans vast and mountains spread.
Children laughed in meadows wide,
Splashing in puddles, side by side.

A kind man and woman, so tender and true,
Stirred feelings within, profound and new.
"I wish to come here," the star child expressed.
"You shall,"said the angel, "but first, you must rest."

Song: "Sleep my little star child,
Sleep the long night through.
While you sleep,
I will weave a coat of light for you."

For days and weeks and months she slept,
While the angel, promises kept,
Wove a coat of light so rare,
For the star child's earthly wear.

"Now it's time," the angel spoke,
As the star child gently awoke.
Dressed in her coat, radiant and bright,
She approached a bridge of rainbow light.
"Take courage," the angel's gentle plea,
As the child crossed over with heart so free.

Song: "In heaven shines a golden star,
An angel brought me from afar,
From heaven high unto the earth,
And brought me to my house of birth."

Variations of a birthday story are told in Steiner-Waldorf kindergartens around the world, to celebrate a child's birthday. Often the parents are invited in and the story is told at the end of the morning session during storytime, just before going home. It is always very moving, and parents are often in tears, deeply touched when they remember the beauty of their child's origin, the echoes of their own origin, and the destiny that is waiting to unfold.

Can you imagine a guardian angel? What if we all have a guardian angel that walked with us as we journeyed to birth and keeps us in the energy of protection as we walk on this earth now?

Simply be invited to use the metaphor—an image of a protective angel—for a mystery that does not need to be put into words. We feel protected by a force of love beyond our finite mind, designed for self-preservation.

You do not have to take on any prescribed thought, but you can open to an image, your own image, and play with a new possibility as you wonder.

Do we have an energy around us of protective love? Is there an energy beyond our physical bodies that lies in mystery and not knowing? How does it feel *not* to know?

We might imagine a certain story and see a guardian angel as the musical conductor of our lives—an angel, or a certain loving energy, that makes sure we meet the right moments and souls, our sacred encounters for our unique assignment in this life. The angel can be seen as the expression or messenger of the original Source, a love that lives within and conveys the wisdom to us, like a bridge, so that we can better hear through the image of love to our heart.

How do we respond? How do we choose to express our unique life's music as a reflection of what is in our hearts? How might we be guided and inspired to act with compassion and care?

In moments of seeking support for another, we can call upon this intuitive guidance to bring exactly what is needed at just the right time.

Can we connect to each other's guardian angels in times of need, especially when seeking to support someone else? Our guardian angels can work together by the simple open invitation we give as we ask for spiritual support.

What if you tried asking your guardian angel to communicate with the guardian angel of your child, your partner, your companion—the one for the other in connection—as you call in a higher loving guidance?

As a parent, a teacher, or anyone close to a child, a whole new view is opened up.

And now, as adults, we are able to reflect on our own arrival on Earth as we also reflect on the essence of any child we are here to guide. With a soft heart space, open to receive, these words could be spoken inwardly as a parent, carer, or teacher:

"Here is a divine child who has chosen to come to Earth with a sacred purpose and is led by an angel.

Here is a human being I do not yet know.

I surrender to the fact that I do not know all the answers.

I embrace the mystery of this unique person or child. I feel reverence for their unique journey. I choose to open to receive inspiration and insight, to come closer and support them with love."

An adult's role and approach then takes on such a different perspective.

For now, it is not so much a question of, "How can I teach a child to become, or shape them to adapt?" but rather

"As I feel awe in the child's presence as they've come fresh from the spiritual world, how can I be of help? How can I be an example—fully human, fully connected to my desire to bring in more love—as the child learns the way of the human in this lifetime?"

Each child, each adult was waiting for the destined meeting. The child at birth in the newness, the freshness, the unknowing, and the forgetfulness from the divine origins of what is to come, asks from the depths of his soul,

"Can I find love again? In your reflection, I know you. Will you recognise me?"

Your place is
Where eyes look at you
Where eyes meet
You come into being
Held by one call
Always the same voice
It is as if there is just one cry
Used by everyone
You could fall
But you don't fall
Eyes catch you
You are here
Because eyes want you
To look at you and say to you
That you are here.

~ Hilde Domin, "You Are Here"

This poem moved me so deeply when it was shared in 2024 at an anthroposophical conference in Dornach, Switzerland.

When eyes meet kindness and love in those who embrace our arrival on earth, a flame in both hearts is lit. When we are received in love, with eyes that recognise the presence of our spirit, the light is invited to integrate deeper within our body. That light fuels our spark of life so that we feel safe to look outward in wonder and openness toward the world, ready and eager.

As a baby, we need the recognition and attention of another for life to take hold in our new body for growth. And so, we begin to realise: we exist here, in this place. The magic of this spark continues to pass between two beings. It shines in the child's eyes as they light up, moving back and forth between parent and child, carried in the luminous connection between our hearts.

This is how the sacred dance of connection begins.

"If Light is in your heart, you will find your way home."

~ Rumi

Did I deserve to be born? Did I choose to be born? How was the news received when my mother discovered she was carrying a new life?

Was it a shock, an inconvenience, embarrassment?

Fear mixed with excitement?

Was I longed for?

Who came before me, and who will come after?

There is reality, and there is our ideal wish for our story.

What if . . .

The stories in my life are the scenes, divinely chosen to realise the true essence of who I am?

The story itself does not matter so much as what I now do in each present moment as it unfolds?

The story is not who I am, is not my true essence?

The story gives me a setting, an environment and an opportunity, and the characters I meet are perfect for the experiences that will occur?

The story is one pathway to remembering as I wake from the dreamy unconscious state of childhood to adulthood?

The dream as a child is an expectation of the ideal mother, the mother figure that embodies all aspects of the Divine Mother who will offer unconditional love for her child.

It is this ideal Mother, the Original Mother, who knows. She will supply all that is needed to support the child's newly incarnated spirit, and in turn the child will be continuously blessed. Yet, what if in actuality the perfectly imperfect mother is the one, the one for each soul that will lead to an experience of deep, universal, felt love?

She was part of our pre-birth agreement, she is here to help us realize the way to bring our gifts to the world, to find our way back home, to know the pain of disconnection, the struggle of misunderstanding, so that we will find our way to fully feel, to fully become aware of the experience of unconditional love—that which is always present and never lost. The human mother, in her weakness and strength, in her joys and suffering, is the one perfect for the story, perfect for us both to fulfil our intertwined destinies and return to our wholeness.

I remember a time when I was busy upstairs and my little daughter was looking for me. She called for me, this time using the word "mother" rather than "mummy," imitating Bambi calling for his mother in the forest (she had just seen the Disney movie). I imagine this moment again, captured in my heart, dreaming in my longings, as though we are led back to see again wider and expanded understandings.

Longings, heartstrings, timelessness.

"Mother, Mother, Where are you? I am looking for you."

Tied together, now and in our sacred contract,
Destined to learn about unconditional love
In the ruptures and the repairs,
In the stark reality of our humanity,
In the squeezing of our hearts,
In our mother's core;
A longing passed down a long line
Only searching for the same unconditional love
From the divine true essence of the Mother figure,

At the core, from the Spirit of Love.

I am the Child, the Mother, the Presence
I want to hear these words:

"Dearest Child,
Know you are loved,
All your dreams are yours.
You are here to dream infinitely.

I am here tc hold your dreams, in hope and joy,
To set you free,
To send you forward in love."

Read these words to reclaim your inner knowing:

I am made of LOVE. And so were my parents. And so are ALL the people I have encountered so far and will encounter in the future.

I choose to come to this place, these parents, this situation—as I am alive in this body. All is for GOOD. I agreed to add transformation to the story, so I can be free to give and receive love here on earth.

If you are asking, *Who am I? Really, at my core, who am I?*—I invite you to say these words to yourself:

"I am Divine.
I am one with the Divine Source that created this body, the spirit
that holds this body with perfect wisdom.
I am here as I am, with every part, made of love for this place,
and deeply loved."

In my experience of finite human form, I contemplate and ask for guidance from the energy of Divine Mother, the Creator of Life, the highest, most Divine Love of universal wisdom—the love we dream of—that every child needs, that the child in you has been searching for.

This Divine Mother energy transcends traditions and names—whether known as Shakti, Sophia, Holy Spirit, or Great Mother—representing the universal feminine principle that births worlds both seen and unseen. She is the sacred container that holds all experience, the embodiment of compassion that sees beyond surface appearances to the divine essence within every being.

It is the energy of a loving Mother who allows and trusts that your own destiny will unfold as is written. She also guards and protects with love and faith, holding you in your connection to your essence.

In the Bible, it is written that Christ says he will send "the Comforter," and *that* is this energy—the essence of a nurturing mother—that holds with tenderness, that lives in us all for eternity. This nurturing presence carries the intuitive wisdom that knows what we need before we can name it ourselves. She speaks the language of the heart, offering guidance that goes beyond intellectual understanding and emerges in moments of surrender.

Can we begin to sense and feel the presence of the Mother within ourselves? To know this lives in our core?

Can we allow ourselves to gently come into Her presence?

Feel into your own being right now.

Notice how this energy feels in your body—perhaps as warmth in your chest, a gentle tingling, or simply a deep sense of peace. The Divine Mother's presence isn't something abstract or distant, but immediately accessible in the body's wisdom, in the breath, in the space between thoughts.

This capacity for nurturing, for creation born of selfless love, is not something you need to work for. It is already here, present in the depths of who you are. Whether you are male or female, young or old, this universal maternal energy flows through us all; it is the breath of life.

Let yourself rest in this awareness.

You are not separate from this miracle of creation—you *are* it, expressed in human form. Right here, right now, you carry within you the same creative power that births stars and galaxies.

Feel the wonder of that truth alive in your body, at this moment, in the eternal now.

No matter how many times we forget, we need not worry; we can reconnect to this loving awareness every time.

Take heart, take hope, for human individuality and our ever moving sense of separation is part of the mystery of divine creation. It is our shared human experience. Let us hold this understanding. It is time to pause, to rest, to breathe…..you are a star!

Allow yourself some time before we begin to explore the childhood stages where needs developed.

From this sacred beginning, I invite you to come further with me. Come, see and feel the treasures we were given to navigate our earthly experience, treasures not yet understood, hidden in the painful experiences, waiting to be lifted up in the joy.

"Stars don't shine because they want to be seen. They shine because they are stars."
~ Alexander Den Heijer "Nothing You Don't Already Know"

CHAPTER 7

AUTHENTIC ATTACHMENT

This above all:
to thine own self be true.
And it must follow, as the night the day,
Thou canst not then be false to any man.

~ William Shakespeare, *Hamlet*

In his book, *The Soul of Discipline*, Kim John Payne outlines three key roles for adults in guiding and supporting children. Anyone who has tried to manage behaviour with children has, at some point, experienced a sense of confusion when experimenting with various ways of regaining a sense of order and control. There are so many books and strategies available for us to try out. And as we shape the child's daily life, we may face opposition, defiance, demands, and what we deem socially unacceptable behaviour. Without full awareness of how to attune to the specific phases of childhood, it's so easy to feel frustrated and anxious.

Just as a garden needs different care through the seasons, children need different forms of guidance as they grow. Understanding developmental phases helps us provide age-appropriate support that honours children's growing capacities while maintaining important loving boundaries that help them feel safe and held.

Payne describes the adult's role as it changes through each phase as **the Governor, the Gardener, and the Guide**. I have found his descriptions of the changing roles very helpful. If we unpack what it means as we evolve with the child, we can receive fascinating insights into how to meet their needs. Understanding these flexible roles also helps us as adults to reflect on what we ourselves needed as children during our different childhood phases and how we might better understand that sense of lack or incompleteness that we feel.

The names Payne gives for our changing roles are particularly helpful because we can use these images to feel into what each loving role might entail. What qualities does a loving Governor have in keeping everyone safe? These roles correspond beautifully to the developing mind: the Governor works with the primitive brain, the Gardener nurtures the limbic emotional brain, and the Guide supports the rational thinking prefrontal cortex as ideas, thoughts, and intellect develop. As a Guide, we guide thoughts in a way that does not dictate the direction.

In the early years, from birth to age 7, the term "Governor"—the one holding the responsibility—creates the secure boundaries and rhythms of daily life that help children feel safe and support their physical and emotional wellbeing. As children move into the middle years, we adults become more like Gardeners, nurturing the children's growing independence and expanding love into the wider world whilst still maintaining the supportive structures that they need.

Finally, during the child's teenage years, we transition to the role of Guide, offering wisdom and partnership as young adolescents try out new ideas and discover their own paths.

We will begin in the first seven years, investigating how our core beliefs about ourselves were formed and how we learnt whether we felt safe to bring our full authentic being into a relationship.

Foundation Senses Focus: Touch, Life, Movement, Balance

Learning Journey Stages: Instinct and Imitation moving toward Imagination

Adult Role/Child Needs: The Governor

During a child's first seven years, the Governor's role is as a loving guardian who creates protected pathways and establishes the structure within which a young child can thrive. The Governor sets loving limits and creates predictable patterns that help children feel at home in an overwhelming world. This isn't about control but about offering the gift of security.

When adults are afraid to set boundaries, believing they might restrict a child's freedom, they often create an unsettling environment where the child feels lost and anxious and constantly tests to find where the edges are. In contrast, a child whose world is lovingly governed experiences a sense of freedom—the freedom to play, explore, and grow without carrying the weight of too many choices or decisions they're not yet ready to make. Through gentle consistency, clear guidance, and a calm presence, the Governor creates the foundation of security from which all healthy development can unfold.

BORN TO CONNECT

As we explored in the previous chapter, our joy and wonder in life began with the essential spark of our first encounter, ignited in the gaze between parent and child. From birth, we are designed to attach and attune to our caregivers for our survival, which is fundamentally dependent on the feelings of love and acceptance we receive. This innate drive to connect—essential to our human existence—reveals how, without real connection as a child, we experience life as though under threat. We become activated deep within the body, ancient survival mechanisms engaging at the most primal level.

The absence of secure attachment triggers physiological responses designed for preserving life itself. Connection is woven into the very fabric of our being. We are focussed on keeping our main caregivers close. For a child, to be disconnected means, "I could die."

BUILDING RELATIONSHIPS

Think of attachment as a baby bird's connection to the nest. The nest—sturdy, carefully woven, and lined with warmth—cradles the fledgling as it grows. When a bird first leaves its nest, it doesn't fly directly into the distant sky. Instead, it makes short flights, always returning to that secure place. With each journey, it flies a little farther, gaining confidence in knowing the nest remains. The parent birds circle nearby, sometimes guiding, sometimes watching, but always present.

So too with children—this "secure base" provides both safety and the courage to explore. A child with a secure attachment explores the world with the inner knowing that the main caregiver is always there to return to. Without this invisible nest—this emotional anchor—a child's explorations are anxious and lack full focus on the new experience. Attention is directed toward the need to stay safe,

As we grow into our adult self, the secure base from childhood opens the door to create an increasing interest in others.

Our first relationship with our parents becomes the blueprint for all future relationships.

We can be securely or insecurely attached. We adapt to the relationship, whatever it takes, when we are so vulnerable and dependent on our adult caregivers.

When it doesn't feel safe to be yourself, an inauthentic attachment style develops. We change ourselves to stay connected. Attachment styles have been described in several ways: anxious, avoidant, disorganized, and our behaviour, especially when we sense danger, will magnify the expressions of the style we have adopted.

Children do not analyze what they need to do to stay attached. The primitive, unconscious part of the brain takes over. The only purpose of the various identities we make for ourselves is to get love, approval, safety, and a sense of belonging.

If we did not experience acceptance for authentic being from the early stages of childhood, the feeling of needing to stay safe overrides the need for authenticity and builds a wall, a falseness, between us and the true being of the other. We create our roles out of this unconscious fear.

This is why we can't really see others for who they are, and we forget who we are at our core.

As a child, I remember a sense of wounding in my own heart: the tightening that occurred deep within when my intentions were misconstrued, when I felt humiliated by being placed at the centre and then ridiculed, showcased in a group, or when my deepest sharings were casually tossed aside. Silenced for fear of speaking up, rooted in fear of provoking the adult's anger or disapproval, I responded with a freezing inward movement: *be still, very quiet. They may not notice you, and then you will be safe. Retreat within, for there you are safer.* And without voicing the feelings or causing a fuss, I could be labelled a "good girl."

The same wounding can rise up at certain moments now, as an adult, triggered in the primitive, unconscious area of my brain. To address a room of many listeners has required great efforts to find courage, time after time.

I know many of us feel this fear. When I first started speaking to audiences—when giving educational talks, for example—I felt frustrated with myself for feeling this debilitating anxiety. My heart beat so fast, palms were sweaty, and I was ready to flee. And of course, I couldn't flee, so then I'd panic about freezing and forget everything I wanted to say.

Underneath all our tactics and behaviours, we are looking for someone who sees who we are, understands what we are trying to communicate, and accepts us as we are. The root of our fear is the sense of disconnection from others, feeling separate, comparing ourselves to both the "worthy" and those we judge as "unworthy."

The archetype of the child holds a picture: the child that needs our love through our attention and our presence so they can grow and develop.

I have found a way to come into a place of less *hard* effort and remember that what I bring to others from connecting to the calm place within will allow all of who I am to feel safer. Everyone is looking for someone real. For me, that's to be more of who I really am and reframe my role as a speaker; to let go of perfection; to connect with my bodily sensations with more compassion; to see how to be of service; to understand the audience is a gift, through the challenge, to lead me back to myself.

We are often validated in society when we present ourselves as independent, in control, achieving human beings. Yet, it is *interdependence*—not the separate energy of independence—that is our natural state.

All this talk of self-regulation that parents are told their children must have, or that is expected in schools, playgrounds, and moments of great challenge, often assumes that adults must have it too. But it is only ever *co-regulation*—for we need each other to truly thrive.

I like to imagine two people practicing music together and working out harmonies. A parent and child's nervous systems attune to each other in a delicate dance. When the child's internal rhythm becomes chaotic or overwhelmed, the adult doesn't simply hand them sheet music and expect them to read it; rather, they join the performance, offering a steady rhythm, a calming tune, until gradually, the child learns to integrate these patterns into their own being. Eventually, they carry this internal music within them, but the strong foundation comes from the countless small moments of shared harmony, not the long periods of isolated practice.

THE DAMAGE OF PUNISHMENT

I planted new trees in my garden in England. I chose them and had a vision for them. They are still delicate, the roots unseen as they seek strength under the soil, and the branches are finding their way upward toward the sky. I also have slightly older trees, also delicate but more formal trees needing to be shaped, and they were planted a few years ago. There is one that was originally very tightly bound to the stake that I did not realise was tightly packed with soil quite high at the base.

When strong winds come, the tightly bound tree can hardly move at all, whereas the other trees have a more gentle support that allows them to sway and move, so they can strengthen their own roots while not becoming completely uprooted. The tree that has grown dependent on the external control has marks and scars where the bindings cut into its growing trunk. It does not produce as many leaves in summer and is the first to lose them in autumn.

The other trees seem to have developed better resilience, the roots growing deeper because they've been allowed to respond to the strong wind within safe boundaries. And then I realised I had to try to work out what was needed, what could be adjusted. I could loosen the tight binding off the restricted tree, even cut some of the binding, and remove some soil that was packed high around the base preventing air circulation. Now I am waiting to see if these adjustments will allow new leaves to grow. Already this summer it is looking a bit healthier.

This story about trees in the garden helps us reflect on boundaries, control, and how as parents we see our role in bringing up our children.

How often do parents unwittingly think they are disciplining for the child's own good when discipline is often associated with punishment? To some people, discipline can mean correction with strict control. The adult's need to control comes from fear and a belief that the child must comply or the adult has failed.

The word "discipline," from the word "disciple," means "to follow the example of someone devoted to their beloved"—one they are pulled toward to follow, to imitate, to love. Therefore, to *discipline* is to lovingly lead, nurture, and guide, like providing that gentle support to the young tree.

When a child is punished—either through exclusion, humiliation, or being made a spectacle of—the threat and fear of rejection, along with the sense of shame, becomes a powerful experience that is held in the body.

Teachers and parents can treat challenging behaviour as though it were part of the child's very essence . . . and a threat to authority. The child's failure to obey can trigger a deep, unconscious fear in the adult.

This creates a fearful child with a fearful adult.

Yes, underneath the adult's anger and frustration is fear. Adults often perceive children's difficult behaviours as a personal attack. Viewing it as a threat to their own self-worth, they are angry at not being respected and are driven to quash it quickly to prevent perceived chaos and further threat.

This is what we may have heard when we were children:

- Go to your room or get out of my sight.
- Time-out Go to the naughty step to "think about what you've done" (impossible for young children whose brains are not developed for rational thinking, so instead, these punishments trigger a disconnection distress and the threat response in the child from fear and an emotional pain from feeling cut off) and then repent.

  In these punishments, the adult is projecting onto the child, "You cause my anger, so I cannot bear looking at you. The message is, "You are unwelcome when behaving this way." The adult believes that inherent worth is dependent on behaviour.
- Face the wall.

  This punishment implies worthlessness: you will not be seen, or you do not deserve to be seen.
- How dare you speak back!

  The message is, "You threaten my authority." The adult is in an unconscious state of fear, triggered, feeling insecure and disconnected from the strong anchor of their being. Control of the child supports their own need to be in control, to avoid the feeling of failure. Without conscious awareness, we may parent our children as we were parented.

- Taking away items or rewarding conditionally.
  This implies, "You must earn my approval. I will control. You must behave accordingly to deserve what I have given you."

Punishment creates fear, stress, and anxiety in the child that will block new learning. Children try to adapt, and when physical behaviour as communication is unheard, they will find it hard to progress to sharing feelings verbally or to develop a more conscious connected form of expression.

New learning comes through the strong presence of an adult who is firmly rooted in their true being and able to role model compassionate connection and communication. Instead of punishment, we can embrace the concept of a more connecting and compassionate approach referred to by Dr. Daniel Siegel as "time in."

Time in offers the connecting alternative to punishment, where adults remain present with children during moments of emotional distress, providing calm support and helping them understand their feelings appropriately without blame or shame. It is helpful to remember that the younger the child the more powerful the force of imitation. Young children need an experience of non-verbal communication where actions and gestures matter.

As adults, our actions and inner state matter more than words. Children under age 7 are the open-sense organs that fully absorb the adult's emotional state—all the gestures and the hidden meaning that creates an energy for change.

Too much talk and rational thinking, overloading with analysis and wordy explanations, cannot reach the deeper levels of the child's being; our lengthy lectures are ineffective. Children up to age 7 in particular absorb unconsciously, yet deep, within the body what brings wisdom and truth for later understanding that provides strength and resilience.

So now we can establish this fact: discipline is *not* punishment. The most loving way, the most effective way, is to help children learn ways to regulate themselves within the calming presence of the adult.

As the child moves toward the middle years, increasing language capacity—new descriptive words for identifying and sharing of feelings—begins to happen naturally. The loud, challenging child is communicating, as is the very shy and withdrawn child, the overly smiling child, the anxious child, or the whining child. They have a message through it all:

"I need to connect with you. Help me restore my sense of balance, my confidence in moving out and onwards, to go into the world, to keep alive a joy for learning."

How many of us, as adults, feel blocked in managing and expressing our emotions? When we are at a loss to help ourselves, for sure we cannot help our children. It seems like an endless, repetitive cycle. We do as was done to us, or we veer way out of balance in acts of avoidance.

In times of stress, we move to autopilot. This is how we may have learnt to manage stress in the unconscious imitative behaviour that we made a part of us, taken from our parents, our families, our significant people who were our role models.

HEALING AND CONNECTION

The guiding principle becomes, *reconnect, not correct.* Challenging or irrational behaviour in both children and adults is a nonverbal cry for help, a physical manifestation of an internal struggle. And when we help our children regulate their feelings, something beautiful happens: we also begin to heal parts of ourselves that once felt unseen.

Conflict is not the end of connection. It is about learning how to be together.

NATURAL LEARNING AND BELONGING IN SCHOOL AND WITHIN FAMILIES

Young children thrive best in environments that mirror natural community settings. Traditional preschool classrooms with same-age groupings and too few adults often create competitive dynamics where young children struggle for attention.

In contrast, mixed-age groups (typically ages 3–6 in preschool and all ages in families) create natural learning communities where younger children learn social skills by observing older ones, while older children develop a flavour of authentic leadership and have a chance to practice nurturing abilities.

This arrangement supports and meets the need for a real sense of belonging cultivating more empathy. As children approach ages 6–7 years, their development allows for them to bring more genuine expressions of care for others, and this is strengthened the more they have been able to imitate the role modelling of caring adults.

The key to nurturing healthy social development—a natural desire for cooperation—always lies in authentic role modeling and attentive adult presence. Rather than forcing behaviours like sharing or showing concern, adults live the principle from their true selves. They guide with gentle wisdom, creating security that allows children's natural capacity for caring to unfold in its own time.

As children develop language and begin actively seeking moral guidance from adults, they can learn to work cooperatively rather than competitively. Same age classes begin to function better, from 6-7, once a child has passed the dreamy stage of imitation.

This approach in the early stages of childhood creates an authentic community - closer to the feeling of an extended family where children develop social skills through natural, meaningful family like relationships rather than rigidly imposed rules where order is placed as the highest priority.

THE PATH FORWARD: CONSISTENCY, PRESENCE, LISTENING

Imagine the loving attention of an adult toward a child as a garden that thrives not through random, heavy, thunderous downpours but through the steady, gentle rain of regular sustenance: consistency, reliability, and natural support in times of need.

In living our lives authentically, from a place of presence, children see how, when we enter a conversation and quickly become distracted by checking our phones or mentally rehearsing our response, we are like a gardener who scatters seeds but never returns to water them. The potential for connection withers before it can take root. But when we offer the clear water of our undivided attention into a relationship, even the most reluctant seeds—the wounded parts, the shy expressions, the trusting shares—begin to unfold and flourish.

What are the ways we will come together for understanding within our families?

Here we come back once again to the powerful force of loving attention —the full attention that we have seen is a form of devotion as we create the space in our hearts to speak and hear our innermost needs. We will allow attention to be the healing medicine. For in this moment between you and me, with my full presence, is the space where new things can be brought to life, where pulsing life is present, waiting to be heard. When we can listen to another as feelings are explored without judgement, and open up to a deeper acceptance and expression of love.

Unconditional love does not take away our freedom to experience all we came here for, and it does not judge, distract, or disempower. In love, we bear with each other, we carry the pain together, and in freedom when we struggle, when we have moments of forgetfulness, we find our practice, and we choose to keep returning to the love that we are.

For children, your listening may be just your quiet, calm presence, your noticing, and your willingness to try to understand.

We can do this for each other. It is in our kindness and care that our relationships are healed. Yet, just as we do not expect children to show care because "we say so," as adults we hold deep reverence for our inner core, bringing our genuine expression of care as it is. This is authentic love and kindness for another—and this is all anyone wants to receive.

For parents struggling with challenging behaviour, for those who remember the damaging effects of the punishment they themselves received, be held with compassion. You are seen.

Find another person, create the space, connect with a listening partner who does not interrupt or correct, who allows you to speak until you can find the space inside you, in the here and now, that has faith for the truth of who you are.

We can learn how to listen at a level we may never have experienced before. We listen to each other *for* each other, and we listen to divine inspiration. Perhaps you will find someone's words that bring healing and more peace for you. Listening to another is a beautiful, loving practice. In Chapter 12, I will share some thoughts and practices that are profoundly healing.

Listening can be full and sacred. It happens over our whole being.

The first level begins with an awareness in our body, built up through this stage of the first seven years, and this bodily awareness is where the foundation of our feeling for truth is formed. This is where we are now.

The second level will connect us through the feelings and emotions in our soul level. This capacity we build most strongly in the middle years (which we will discover in Part Two).

The third level connects us in our thinking, to pause our own thoughts, to recognise those stuck thoughts and the creative thoughts with increasing awareness, to try and understand those of another (which we will explore in Part Three).

We explore the coming together of these three levels to reach the highest capacity for sacred listening—the fourth level (which will be shown in Chapter 12). This is the moment when we are open to hearing beyond our own story, when we let go of our feelings, likes, dislikes, and limited opinions and ask to connect to the source of a greater wisdom. In this place of listening we receive inspirations for the highest good of the whole.

And so for now, let us return to base to see how these first seven years shape and model the vessel that we need, to see what influenced us at this time of our lives, to feel what we can do now to regain a loving, trusting connection to our bodies, to support our children, and to hear and use the body's wisdom as the foundation for our greatest potential.

CHAPTER 8

THE ARCHITECTURE
OF BEING

"We are bees, and our body is a honeycomb.
We made the body; cell by cell we made it."

~ Rumi

Have you had the experience of really tuning into your body? We can find today many practices of embodied awareness. Have you ever said or thought, "I feel it in my body as truth"?

In the freshness of childhood, our bodies are designed to open and take in an experienced sense of truth, storing it not as intellectual concepts but as living wisdom within the very cells of our being. Like an ancient library in which each volume contains not just words but living memories, the body archives every experience—each gesture, sound, and sensation—creating a holder of truth that will serve us throughout life.

The body speaks a language more primal and honest than words could ever express. Across cultures and throughout history, wisdom traditions have honoured this embodied knowing. Ancient practices like qigong recognise that our physical form possesses an inherent intelligence about movement and healing that existed long before our rational minds developed conceptual understanding. These movement arts from Eastern traditions support a profound connection between breath, intention, and physical form, helping restore our natural capacity for presence.

Indigenous healing systems worldwide acknowledge the body's inherent wisdom as inseparable from our spiritual and emotional wellbeing. Traditional healing approaches integrate the body, soul, and spirit rather than treating them separately. These ancestral practices remind us that healing is restored in a harmony between body, community, and environment.

In this chapter, as we explore the architecture of our physical being, we'll discover how this bodily foundation established in our earliest years creates the vessel through which life flows. Through returning to the body's wisdom, we reconnect with an intelligence that precedes thought and becomes our compass back to presence when the mind has wandered far away from home.

Permission to Move

Now I practice this sensation of movement,
my soft body ready to be formed,
to be shaped into what I will become.
My body moves, guided with an invisible drive.

For movement begins
and my own consciousness must slowly awaken.
My eyes look for yours; is this safe?
Free movement, you let me,
And hold me in your consciousness
in your smile or your frown,
your anxiety, or your distraction,
detected by the vibrating mirror neurons,
in the resonance and the micromovements of your body
Inextricably linked with my permission to practice.
I am the sponge,
and your centredness is my starting block
My reach out to touch, to grasp this thing I see,
This thing I feel with my body;
Do you know, when I move as my body tells me,
I am building self-confidence for the future?
To know I can do it
When you allow me to repeat, over and over,
I will perfect my instrument.
Give me time.
No need to fear, I can do this.
I build my will.
My body knows,
My body is a miracle,
My body holds the truth
In this moment,
For my human becoming.

The child under age 7 (in particular) moves through innate intuition, is driven to move, to do, to be in action, and needs to have movements to imitate.

> *"We speak of Truth, little realizing that a feeling for truth is connected with our consciousness of the physical body."*
> **~ R. Steiner, "Truth, Beauty and Goodness" (GA220 lecture, January 19, 1923)**

This we now know: the first seven years of life establish the foundation upon which a person's entire future development will rest. Children are indeed architects of their growth and build their understanding of the world piece by piece.

In this chapter, we will see how these first seven years are crucial to the foundation of our future development, and we will come to realize how the physical senses create solid ground for both a healthy sense of self and the body's ability to sense truth. We will discover how authentic early experiences build a child's basic trust in the world, and how we allow the body's natural intelligence to guide the process of physical development as we are building strength for the future.

Are we, as adults, able to tune in to the body's messages and honour what needs to be heard?

Can we hear our own truth and feel it in the body's knowing?

Can we distinguish our own felt truth and that of another?

How was our bodily truth shaped during the first seven years of life?

THE POWER OF AUTHENTIC MOVEMENT

During these foundational years, children are natural seekers of truth, driven from within to explore the essence of all things both living and material in the world. They explore their environment as dedicated investigators who absorb every experience deeply, storing them as resources in the body. Each sensation they encounter transforms into embodied knowledge that shapes their physical form as they grow.

In the body, guided by innate developmental wisdom, sensory foundations are built that will later support mature thinking, feeling, and strength of will. It is these foundations that enable us to act freely, to choose in adulthood that which comes from the innate connection to spiritual goodness, felt as truth in the body

Every gesture, every touch, every movement shapes not just the physical form but the very foundation of how a child will come to know themselves and their place in the world.

I had the opportunity and privilege to attend training at the Pikler Institute in Budapest and learn from Anna Tardos, the daughter of Dr. Emmi Pikler. There are two main principles of Pikler's methods for supporting the healthy development of the young child from birth to age 3:

1. Authentic relationship

2. The child's freedom for self-initiated movement

It was a wake-up call for me to realize how much adults physically manipulate children without awareness.

We think we need to teach a child to walk! We buy contraptions and gadgets, we hold our children's hands in the air, thinking we are helping, yet they can't experience their own sense of balance or know the sensation of self-movement. Whilst this may bring us pleasure as adults, it helps us to also acknowledge that we may be carrying some anxiety around our roles too; we want to help them excel early, and we are eager for them to move on. We think they need us to teach them, and we believe we are assisting them.

> *"Be careful what you teach. It might interfere with what they are learning."*
> ~ **Magda Gerber, *Dear Parent: Caring for Infants with Respect***

We sit children up before they are ready because we are also keen to conform to the norm: it's what others do, and we are confused by outside seemingly professional information.

Pikler's work is powerful, ongoing, and has flourished around the world, enabling thousands of children and families to build healthy, connected lives. Pikler's teachings have expanded from her modeling for the caregivers at the original orphanage in Budapest how to slow down, connect, work with children in partnership, and support the babies and toddlers who faced the tragic loss of their parents in the war. This approach has now taken root in many institutions globally that pass on loving guidance to families in day care centres, nurseries, and support groups.

In these precious first first years of life, truth is not an intellectual concept; it is a lived, bodily experience. It is an innate drive that resonates as a felt sense of truth rather than intellectual awareness or analysis in the brain.

In all the bodily senses, a little child *feels* the way to connect to the essence of everyone and everything, practicing with the body in space, repeating and perfecting the skills, coming into the upright, and taking steps to begin walking.

Children touch all the objects of the world to learn *what is me, what is the essence of the thing I touch, who is touching me*?

The child is driven onwards by the gifts of the spirit, an instinctual wisdom, propelled forward and in all dimensions through the unconscious forces of the will.

As we come to see that how we are formed is shaped by our environment, we also need to recognise that the most important glue that holds us together in childhood is our relationship, our deep connection with a trusted person. The relationship with a key person is the only thing that matters to the child. From this safe point, a natural expansion outward flows.

THE POWER OF IMITATION

In the mirroring of our main caregivers—the actions, the gestures, the sounds of language—the body is shaped and formed. The effects of the sights, sounds, and movements echo and go right into the substance of the physical organs.

That we imitate is a gift from the spiritual world. For a child, imitation is a practice of devotion to the main caregivers. Imitation is the beginning inward experience, resonating and vibrating for connection and relationship.

This is the unconscious, deeply felt experience for the young child:

I feel how you are feeling, I move how you move, for I vibrate within as the reflection of your soul lights me up or closes me down.

The mind that connects what we do with who we are at our core is formed from stored memories and the images we make because our role models described us and reflected back to us their own sensed perception. Like a sponge, we absorb and take it all in. We were designed to learn that way. In this early stage of life, our bodies stock up the experiences that will be called upon in the future.

Children in the first seven years are looking for true reflections of human life. They do not feel the drudgery of housework, the annoyances the adult feels in the ritual of the caregiving—expressed in language, gestures, sighs, and complaints—but children do begin to absorb it as a way of being.

For a child, as we work in the home or garden, caring for things for others is fascinating, alive. We are giving them a picture of how we care for and love each other and the environment. There is so much variety and so much we can do: repairing, cleaning, cooking, gardening, building, making things, welcoming people into our lives with warmth.

Without seeing adults in genuine everyday action, without a safe relationship, children begin imitating whatever they can find in their environment. This could be other children, animals, or even machines.

They are especially drawn to the images and actions of characters made by adults for the screen or in children's books. We think this is helping children's imagination, but these characters are not developed from the child's own internal processes.

Children at this early stage of development seek true representations of the world around them. When encountering images for the first time, they can be affected by the exaggerated and unrealistic portrayals that adults create in their own imaginations. The garish colours and mechanical characteristics often applied to animals or humans—frequently blurring the distinction between the two—can create subtle or not so subtle stress in children. This distortion, though sometimes difficult to detect, can disconnect children from authentic life experiences and hinder their natural understanding of the world.

There is so much to reflect on as we think about what our children are exposed to: the images on the screens and the behaviour of adults. It is good to reflect on this. It is good to become more aware.

Imitation without authentic connection to another human becomes stuck in the body on repeat and cannot release into a stage of new learning.

I have often seen this in the kindergarten where children become obsessed with TV characters. These fixed images that are not of their own imagination keep them stuck in repetitive, imitative patterns, and they struggle to play creatively with fresh ideas that would uniquely and deeply serve them in all areas of their development.

Only through witnessing real, purposeful, human activity can children move forward from the deep imitation stage to include, develop and produce the fluid, creative, imaginative ideas that support their natural development.

PHYSICAL CARE AS SOUL NOURISHMENT: SENSE OF LIFE & WELL-BEING

We have explored how, from the very first relationships of our early childhood we began to form a constructed sense of self based on the warmth of the love and physical care we received. The way we are cared for in the first seven years translates as nourishment that feeds our budding sense of self.

This is what we discovered from Chapter 6: *the physical care I receive, given in tenderness and with warm attention or in contrast with coldness and distraction, affects my sense of worthiness.*

If I feel the sense of "me" in the reflection of your eyes and in your gestures, then how your hands touch me, how you care for my life body (my sense of well-being), how your feelings are transmitted so subtly in your facial expressions, the tone in the sounds in your words, and your actions will help me feel safe, seen, and valued.

How am I touched? Am I allowed to move? Do you have confidence in my movement? Do you make me move in unnatural ways? Do you have trust in my body's unique pace and wisdom? These questions speak to the fundamental experience of developing a sense of self and well-being.

When we bring in a sense of safety through a gentle, organised environment —predictable patterns for each day, and reliable, soul-nourishing rituals—the whole being of the child can feel safe, cared for, and regulated from within. This is also particularly important in the middle phase of life (as we will see in Part Two) where the security and regularity that the body relies on creates a flowing, healthy circulatory system. In the flow of our bodily processes, feelings are also able to move and flow. We are connected in our heart realm through the processes of breathing, circulation of bodily fluids and pumping of blood.

Key Takeaways

We looked at how the first seven years of life are foundational for all that follows.

- When given time and space in nurturing environments with loving adults who prioritise doing things together, children build deep bodily security *and* trust in the world.

- Young children learn primarily through doing and experiencing, not intellectual instruction. We can design environments around this developmental reality.

- True freedom develops within appropriate safety limits based on the child's developmental needs, not on adult conditioning, unmet dreams, or projections.

- These protective boundaries allow for the delicate unfolding of the child's being, fostering bodily felt truth and enabling the whole self to flourish.

Security & Trust Needs (0–7 Years)

During these foundation years, a child requires:

- physical safety and security;
- warm, nurturing bodily care;
- development of basic trust;
- a sense of being protected and held;

- experience of movement and loving touch; and

- consistent, reliable presence from caregivers.

Impact of Unmet Needs

When these fundamental needs go unfulfilled, a profound gap forms that follows us into adulthood, manifesting as:

- relentless reassurance-seeking—constantly hunting for external validation and comfort that never truly satisfies the internal void;

- protective self-aggrandisement—creating façades of importance to shield against deep-seated feelings of inadequacy and unworthiness;

- pervasive suspicion—approaching relationships defensively, always scanning for threats, making genuine connection nearly impossible; and

- cycles of betrayal—repeatedly finding oneself in relationships characterised by broken trust, either as the betrayed or betrayer, unconsciously recreating original patterns of unreliable care.

In recognising these patterns, in becoming conscious of these deep longings, we find the first key to our healing. The first steps are to simply become aware, to recognise, to hold, to listen; and then to open with curiosity.

Healing Meditation

I am inviting you to listen to a meditation I created for you to help heal these early wounds of safety and trust. Through these words, you will hear the loving reassurance your body has been longing for. Let your adult self become the protective presence your younger self needed as we restore, together, your foundation of deep security and trust.

Truth in the Body: A Healing Meditation

Take a deep breath and settle comfortably. Allow yourself to be fully present as these words find their way to the little child within you who longs to be seen and held.

"Dearest love, at this moment, I am here with you. Can you feel the ground beneath you, holding you completely?

Your body is a vessel of wisdom that has carried you faithfully through every moment of your journey.

The truth of your body was always enough.

You were always worthy of tender care, of being touched with reverence, of being seen with eyes of wonder.

You were that little one who needed safety and protection.

And, my love, you are seen.

You can feel it now: feel the love of the Mother who is always with you.

Feel the warmth spreading through your limbs, a reminder that you are completely held.

Your very existence is a miracle that needs no justification.

The child in you who longed to feel safe and secure is being held closely now.

Your body holds memories, yes, but it also holds freedom.

With each breath, receive what was always your birthright.

Now you will begin to feel more and more at home in your body.

You open, release, relax—slowly.

You trust in your body's wisdom.

You will know deep security.

You are safe. You are held. You are home.

This is the truth your body has always known.

Rest in this knowing, pause here, breathe slowly, and know it is yours, always, infinitely: your true resting place"

We have seen how the physical body lays the roots in the quality of the "soil" that is provided—in the experience of truth that is absorbed and imitated.

Here we have the ground laid for the next stages.

As we look ahead to the next phase of childhood, from ages 7 to 14, we feel the transition and the shift.

The energy that has been primarily focussed on physical development begins to move and expand. The child who was once fully absorbed in the world of physical activity and "will forces" now, over time, begins to deepen awareness of the world of feelings and emotions.

Just as the first seven years laid the foundation through the four basic senses, this next phase opens up the heart forces, bringing new capacities for feeling and emotional understanding.

Their expressions of empathy and emotional understanding deepen whilst the active "doing" of the bodily actions becomes more conscious and deliberate.

Now, we are ready. We will enter the middle years of childhood to discover how these bodily foundations support the flowering of a "feeling life," appreciation of beauty, and love of others and the world.

PART
TWO

BEAUTY IN THE SOUL
AGES 7–14

"Since love grows within you, so beauty grows. For love is the beauty of the soul."

~Saint Augustine

Middle Senses Focus: Warmth, Sight, Smell, Taste

Learning Journey Stages: Imagination to Innovation

Adult Role/Child Needs: The Gardener

For children aged 7–14, the Gardener, shifting into a new way of relating, provides a nurturing environment where a child's sense of self-worth can take root and flourish. At this stage, children are highly sensitive to how they are seen by the adults around them. The Gardener sees and appreciates the child's inner sense of beauty, fostering self-confidence and a natural ability to relate to others with love and care. Instead of criticism and correction, the Gardener offers encouragement and example, guiding children toward growth while ensuring they feel safe and valued.

Through patience, warmth, consistency, a loving presence, and sensitive support the Gardener helps children develop empathy and a deeper connection to their own inner beauty and goodness. Through this gentle yet steady tending, children develop a deep-rooted confidence, knowing they are valued for who they truly are, which in turn inspires them to see and honour the beauty in others. When we provide the right conditions—sunlight, water and our presence—the brighter the blooms of the flower will become. As the Gardener, we do not decide what the flower will look like; we only need to provide unconditional love and care, with no expectations of outcome.

Between the ages of 7 and 14, beauty, emotion, and imagination become the guiding forces that shape the child's unique understanding of the world.

It is here, in this phase, that the heart begins to awaken, and the soul's light can expand outward with interest. When we are supported by adults who model warmth and interest, we are led with warm enthusiasm to learn how to love. It is as though our key adults allow in the sunlight for the upward shoots to grow longer and more vibrant.

I like this image of the plant opening its new leaves to the sun. As in the 12 senses from chapter 5 , the image helps me imagine the soul of the child that now yearns for beauty, connection, and the deep satisfaction of feeling understood. In this middle realm between bodily knowing and intellectual understanding, we find the space of the heart as the child is allowed to grow toward the best and unique path for their life.

In the chapters that follow, we'll explore how this heart space manifests in both the individual emotional life and in the social connections of the child. As we begin, let us look more deeply at how this awakening unfolds and transforms the child's experience of both themselves and the world around them.

We are ready to explore a time when the essence of who we are begins to dance with more conscious awareness of the beauty of life and the awakening to the flow of our emotions. I invite you to reconnect with the eternal essence of your soul, to honour the role of imagination in shaping your life, and to awaken to the beauty that flows through every moment.

Let us step through this door and find this pathway into the heart of what it means to feel, to imagine, and to grow in a sense of connection to each other and to the world.

CHAPTER 9

THE HEART SPACE
AWAKENS

"May warmth of heart keep your presence aflame."
~ John O'Donohue, "For Presence" in *To Bless the Space Between Us*

THE AWAKENING OF BEAUTY AND FEELING

As the physical foundations of the first seven years stabilize, a new dimension of consciousness begins to unfold in the child. Where once the child was primarily engaged with physical activity and sensory exploration, we see how the inner landscape of feelings and emotions takes centre stage. This shift reveals an important transformation in how children relate to the world and to others.

This developmental phase brings expanded capacities: increased memory, a new relationship with time, the ability to form mental pictures independently, and a growing awareness of the self as distinct from others. The focus shifts from *what* things are to *how* things feel to us and affect us emotionally.

The energy that was primarily focussed on physical development now expands, moving upwards, transforming and entering a rich world blending inner experience and outer connection. This transition typically begins between ages 5 and 7, marked by the loss of baby teeth and subtle changes in how children relate to the world around them.

BEAUTY AS SOUL NOURISHMENT

The Soul's Bridge Between Inner and Outer

The soul's feelings and the middle senses—warmth, sight, taste, and smell—serve as bridges between our inner experience and the outer world. Beauty becomes an echo of the Divine, allowing us to feel all our emotions and expand our hearts. The soul is the balancing point between the spiritual world and the world of matter.

Through experiences of nature's beauty, stirrings are ignited deep within the heart. These middle senses lead us into this world of feeling and imagination. Poetry, music, story, food, nature, and all the arts become healing forces for the emotions.

The child takes their cue from the adult. A love for other people, a warm interest in the world, non-judgement, and curiosity for new experiences are supported by the example of our key people. When we as adults appreciate and love the beauty of the world and see all things with openness rather than a critical viewpoint, we help shape and strengthen children's natural capacity to perceive and create beauty for themselves.

SEEING WITH THE HEART

With sight, we take in the light, yet we make our own interpretations of the images. Do we really see what is before us? With an open heart, we allow ourselves to see more of what is there. Our thinking remains fluid and clear when we see with eyes of love.

> *"How is it that we can be so mistaken in the use of our eyes? It is because we 'think in our eyes.' . . . With our thinking, we add what we expect to see to what we actually do see."*
>
> **~ A. Soesman, *Our Twelve Senses***

THE FLOW OF FEELINGS

In our heart space, if love was given only conditionally, or if we were punished with exclusion for behaviours that could not be received or supported by our adults (as we explored in the first seven years), we may have grown to feel unworthy of love. This sense of unworthiness can lead us to constantly search for reassurance in our relationships as we create false images of ourselves to impress others.

When we are allowed to feel and express emotions fully, they remain healthy. However, when we are not permitted to experience them, they become trapped, distorted, and disconnected. Emotions can be felt throughout the body, triggered by thoughts held in the mind and memories stuck in this stage of our childhood that, instead of allowing us to experience joy and hope, keep us feeling trapped in the past.

As our feelings are connected to the circulation of the body and the middle parts of our human form, we can experience where our heart beats faster or slower, our blood flow leaves us pale or rosy, and where our breathing changes. Our body is always seeking to regain balance.

THE ELEMENTS OF EMOTION

Our feelings express all elements of our human nature; in our temperaments we have the heaviness of the earth, the lightness, joy and excitement in air, the fluidity of water that brings soothing, and the fiery passion of intense emotion.

At its core, anger is fear—a fear of not being able to express ourselves authentically or be seen for who we are. When we avoid the pain of grief, for example, and do not allow all to be held, we can also experience anger, leaving us swinging between powerful emotional states of grief, anger, and fear. If we are nurtured in our grief, if we are held by others and allowed to hold space for it, anger and fear can naturally dissolve and will, in their own time, through the power of our presence, give way to compassion.

This compassion extends beyond personal experience to embrace the universal human emotions that connect us all.

We can find support in navigating the ebbs and flows of our emotional realm by establishing healthy rhythms in daily living. This means intentionally creating moments of pause and connection for our children while thoughtfully structuring the activities and schedules that shape our lives. Healthy rhythms to the day regulate breathing, restore steady heartbeats, create a feeling of safety.

RHYTHMS AND CYCLES OF THE HEART

Just as the Gardener ensures the right balance of activity and rest for growing plants, we can establish rhythms that nourish the child's emotional life and strengthen their sense of security and belonging. When we align with the natural world—moving in harmony with sunrise and sunset, acknowledging the cycles of seasons—in our everyday routines, we create a natural balance between active engagement and restorative rest. This balance, tailored to both the developmental needs of the child and the wider needs of the family, helps establish reliable patterns for nourishment, conversation, exploration, and renewal. It is within these rhythmic, connected moments that we receive the essential nurturing that fosters harmony and cultivates more peace.

The balance of activities allows for a healthy breathing in and breathing out. Our breath can become a source of regulation for our nervous systems. Children rely on adults to help with planning the balance of their lives throughout their childhood.

In relationships, our sense for warmth and coldness in feelings is like the warmth or coldness reflected in the cycles of the earth. Like the breathing in of winter and the breathing out of summer, all the colours of coolness and warmth are reflections of our inner being and can be enjoyed for the uniqueness of their beauty.

Like the warmth of connection and the coldness of isolation in relationships, we physically respond to temperature, and our hearts respond to the emotional climate around us—warming in the presence of acceptance and chilling in the face of rejection.

THE MEDICINE OF SEASONAL RHYTHMS

Honouring the rhythms of life nourishes the circulatory system of the body, helping us breathe with a flow and giving us a felt experience of balance over a longer period of time.

The return of the festivals and the seasons each year brings us comfort, security, and a sense of belonging. They are the expression of the beautiful divine creation. We can bring them into our lives and homes very simply. We have to live them to feel them. Even just becoming aware of the four elements helps us create an authentic, beautiful atmosphere that deeply nourishes us and every member of the family in a home. It is a soul nourishing activity for everyone as we create colour, mood and scents within the home to bring in the elements of nature, reflecting the season, and connecting our life within and our time outside in the natural world.

- **Spring**: air—the newness of life, gentle, delicate, emerging, and the freshness of the breeze
- **Summer**: fire—the heat of the sun, the fullness of growth and life, the pinnacle of outward expression as inner consciousness rests
- **Autumn**: earth—the spirit of harvest, abundance, mature, richness, allowing and letting go
- **Winter**: water—the rain, snow, and ice, inner consciousness awakens quietly, building unseen strength for the future.

THE ARTS AS HEART NOURISHERS

During the middle childhood stage in my life, I loved poetry that spoke to feelings so profound they sometimes took my breath away. In the words of the poets I discovered in the old poetry books passed down to me, I found a deep connection with nature and with the deep peace and wonder of the world.

The words helped me recognise the depth of the feelings that filled my new inner life, and I felt comforted that this was a human experience shared with another (the poet). And I revelled in the aching sadness, longing, and yearnings. It was as though these words echoed a recognition of something timeless and true that I deeply felt inside me. And the words soothed the overwhelm; I was not alone.

"Our longing for God is God's love for us. It is the gravitational pull of our being inviting us to return from the adventure of experience to the sanctuary of the heart. Our longing never finds what it is looking for; it comes to rest in it."

~Rupert Spira, *The Heart of Prayer*

Poetry, story, music, and nature therefore become medicine for an overwhelm of emotions. In these arts, we forget our limited self for a while; our own thoughts cease as we unite with what feels like deep universal wisdom.

SUMMER MEMORIES: THE FELT EXPERIENCE OF BEAUTY

Below are some of my childhood memories of the summer season. These memories are held within, yet they feel free and flowing, not fixed and stuck. I see them as soul food.

Summer afternoons spent shelling peas in the back garden, green treasures popping from their pods straight into my mouth.

Cotton sheets on beds, no need for layers of woolly blankets.

Open windows to sleep by while bees hovered between dahlias and roses that painted the garden in wild colours.

The endless light stretched our days into forever. Crawling on hands and knees through secret tunnels in the long grasses. Ice cubes clinking in glasses of lemonade. Sun-warmed cucumbers and tomatoes filling our salad sandwiches.

The sound of the ice cream van's music box song making its way down the street as I clutched the loose change given by my father.

Summer nights whispered with fading light, the air still sweet with memories of the day.

The cliffs and the sea, long holidays in Cornwall.

Memories made of salty sprays, wiry long grass on the cliff tops interspersed with sand. The steep, winding walks down cliffs to the beach. The warmth of spongy grass behind the dunes, lying there looking up at the endless blue sky streaked with the white wisps of angels's wings. The screech of seagulls. The bliss of my solitude on these cliff tops, not loneliness but a deep connection to an inner life of both the earth and the ocean.

The smooth and jagged steely grey rocks carved by the sea's power. The vast, wide, open unknown of the sea. The warm rock pools, silent creatures scurrying beneath the sand. My father—man of the seashores. Wet, wild winds. Long, endless days, feeling weather-beaten, sandwiches on beach towels, tea in flasks, fold-up chairs for Grandma's buckets, wet skin, growing tanned limbs. Aliveness.

THE POWER OF POETRY

I remember learning a poem by heart at this time in my life; I think it was to recite in school. I loved every moment of dreaming into this poem. It felt so real. It has stayed with me long into my later years, and the echo of the memory brings me a feeling of deep connection to the coast, and to the shared knowing present within us—our shared humanity—and a sense of peacefulness.

"Sea Fever" by John Masefield

I must go down to the seas again, to the lonely sea and the sky,
And all I ask is a tall ship and a star to steer her by;
And the wheel's kick and the wind's song and the white sail's shaking,
And a grey mist on the sea's face, and a grey dawn breaking.

I must go down to the seas again, for the call of the running tide
Is a wild call and a clear call that may not be denied;
And all I ask is a windy day with the white clouds flying,
And the flung spray and the blown spume, and the sea-gulls crying.

I must go down to the seas again, to the vagrant gypsy life,
To the gull's way and the whale's way where the wind's like a whetted knife;
And all I ask is a merry yarn from a laughing fellow-rover,
And quiet sleep and a sweet dream when the long trick's over.

I still have goosebumps when I read this poem! I feel taken back to the seas as though I can truly feel and imagine being there again. I feel the presence of my father in this poem, as he grew up close to the sea and always loved returning there. I am taken back to the beauty of the sound of the words as I practised speaking them in my room, evoking the deep presence I felt gazing out over the sea.

SUPPORTING THE HEART'S DEVELOPMENT

As children mature, the level of support needed from the different focus of Governor, Gardener, and Guide changes as the organisation of the children's daily and weekly activities change. As adults, by changing and adapting our roles, we are seeing children's needs more clearly, and they naturally feel more seen and supported.

It is so helpful to keep reminding ourselves that what we need most at all stages of our lives is someone who can witness our pain, challenges, as well as joys without dismissing them, subduing them or trying to fix them. We need someone who says, "I can hear anything you have to say, and I will bear it with you. I am here to love all parts of this moment, not to focus on taking away from you what we may not yet understand but to be alongside you and hold it with you."

When we attune ourselves fully, we naturally develop the discernment to recognise when to step back and allow, when to walk alongside, when to protect, and how to offer meaningful support. The fundamental intention becomes simple yet profound: to avoid becoming an obstacle in another's unfolding journey, whether for a child discovering their path or anyone whose experience we are privileged to witness and accompany.

This middle phase of childhood lays essential foundations for emotional resilience and authentic connection with others. Through the experiences, relationships, and rhythms of these years, children develop their capacity to feel deeply and respond authentically. When our feelings are nurtured in this middle phase, new capacities emerge. By awakening to emotions and moving into the world with feeling, we develop in accordance with the natural law of our growth.

The more adults model compassion and non-judgement, the freer children are to express their feelings, share their experiences, and learn to love others.

THE ETERNAL CHILD WITHIN

"Oh how God loves the child! And gives us all an eternal child with whom we effervescently, everlastingly rebirth, and rebirth our scintillating joy!"

~ Pete Walker, *The Tao of Fully Feeling*

In adulthood, as we remember pleasurable moments from this stage of childhood when we were connected through our imagination with nature, with home rhythms, with our inner life, and with all the new connections we made with others, we feel deeply strengthened and know the experience of joy in life.

Our intention now can be to choose activities that bring renewed joy and comfort to our senses, like walking in nature, cooking favourite meals with their aromas filling the house from seasonal foods and scents, bringing in flowers and objects collected from our walks to decorate special spaces, making crafts, and painting. We can once again reach the heart, reconnect to the joys we allow ourselves to feel in our eternal child to reconnect with awe and gratitude for merely being alive.

As we embrace the beauty that nourishes our hearts through nature, creativity, and simple joys, we can be gently reminded that this inner harmony is also a reflection of the relationships we form with others.

Just as we cultivate joy within ourselves, we begin to recognise how these practices deepen our connection to the wider world, enriching our interactions and allowing us to bring our authentic selves into community. It is through this dance of self-expression and connection that we find our place in the social realm, creating a dynamic balance between who we are and how we relate to those around us.

CHAPTER 10

THE SOCIAL HEART

"A healthy social life is found only, when in the mirror of each soul the whole community finds its reflection, and when in the whole community the virtue of each one is living."

~ R. Steiner, quoted in *The Fundamental Social Law: Rudolf Steiner on the Work of the Individual and the Spirit of Community*

How can we fully express our individuality while still respecting the needs of the wider community? Is this not a question for the whole of our life?

How do we balance our sense of self with the unique path of the other? Reflecting on this as a daily practice shapes not just our thoughts but our real actions in the world, bringing lasting change to how we live with each other. Between ages 7 and 14, the heart of the child opens to the social world in entirely new ways. No longer merely imitating those around them, they begin to feel their way into relationships, developing the emotional intelligence that will serve them throughout life.

MODELLING SOCIAL CONNECTION

How do our children learn to move gracefully in the social world? It's not from our words of instruction but through witnessing our living examples. When we, as adults, bring our authentic selves into each encounter—present, open-hearted, willing to be seen in our truth yet mindful of others—we create an invisible template that shapes our children's understanding of what it means to be in relationship with another. Children instinctively orient toward these genuine examples of human connection they observe in their daily lives, absorbing the subtleties of social wisdom through our every interaction.

The family becomes the first gathering place where social learning takes root. In the simple rhythms of sharing meals together, in how we speak to one another during moments of disagreement, in the small gestures that acknowledge each person's unique gifts and contributions—here is where children absorb the art of being both themselves and part of something larger. When they see us extend our circle of care beyond our immediate family to neighbours or those in need, they experience firsthand how the warmth of community enriches rather than diminishes individual life. The question becomes not, "What social skills should we teach?" but rather, "How are we living, day by day, in the delicate dance between honouring our own truth and nurturing our shared humanity?" For in this balance lies the heart of a truly social life.

PARTNERSHIP IN RELATIONSHIP

Relationships are a dance of giving and receiving that transforms both partners. The true essence of connection doesn't exist within either person but pulses in the space between us, in every exchange of energy, attention, and understanding.

What we discover through relationships reveals our deepest truths; they become mirrors reflecting parts of ourselves we couldn't otherwise see. These connections form the foundation of our human experience, shaping not only how we relate to others but how we co-create meaning, purpose, and beauty in the world. In the delicate balance between independence and togetherness, we find both our uniqueness and our belonging.

As adults, we often expect children to become independent far too quickly. We tell them to get dressed, put on their shoes, and handle tasks on their own, not always out of necessity but sometimes because we yearn for them to grow up.

Yet, what children truly need—and what will help them reach their fullest potential—is the experience of partnership. When we do things *with* a child, rather than asking them to manage alone, we nurture their social heart. This shared effort builds connection and trust. Paradoxically, the less we push children to do things independently, the sooner they naturally assert their autonomy with confidence, saying, "I can do it myself."

Children need adults to actively engage with them, not just shouting out instructions from across a room nor resenting them needing help but guiding them through connection rather than imposing through pressure or shame. This dynamic of doing things together creates the foundation for a more lasting sense of self-empowerment which continues to influence the child later in life.

Feelings of being left too frequently to cope alone leave us feeling unworthy and uneasy about asking for help. When we are pushed toward independence too soon and left to navigate challenges without support, independence can feel less like a choice and more like a survival mechanism—a response rooted in fear, not joy. This push to independence can often happen with the arrival of a new sibling, or when the adult feels anxious about returning to work or simply is exhausted and unable to find support.

The sense of isolation often stays with us into adulthood. While independence has its value, the absence of joy that comes from doing things alone points to the deeper issue of a lack of connection.

A compulsion to be self-reliant can be traced back to childhood experiences where we were forced to take on responsibilities beyond our emotional capacity. Any premature independence may support an adult's feeling that they are teaching their child for the future, but it can leave a child without the nurturing they need during critical developmental stages. Over time, this can lead to the child losing trust in others and developing a deeply ingrained belief that relying on anyone else is unsafe.

Healing can take many forms: reconnecting with the body through movement, mindfulness, or meditation; re-engaging with life's beauty through creative expression; being really listened to; or simply rediscovering the joy of being supported by others by allowing ourselves to take a risk with more trust.

With this awareness—and with support—we can bring a great sense of appreciation to ourselves by connecting with what we already have: the beauty freely available in the natural world, gratitude for the people who support and love us, and the possibilities we can find that inspire enthusiasm for life. By focussing on what we have, we begin to fill the gaps created by earlier experiences of lack. And when this is a struggle for us, we must be kind and gentle with ourselves. We always have a place to return to: the place of noticing, allowing, and holding, then letting the experiences move through our body, giving the time that is needed.

By sharing our stories with those who understand, we create the kind of mutual connection that we longed for. With trusted friends as listeners, we can explore how it feels to share memories, access new ways of being, and "try on" what it feels like to be given the time we need now for support.

And, as a devoted listener for another, with trust in *their* own wisdom, we can help them feel confidence and trust to speak their truth, to cope when they are ready.

By revisiting this stage of childhood and addressing the unmet needs for connection and partnership, we begin to understand the wounds that shaped us. In doing so, we strengthen and transform our social heart and rediscover the joy of shared effort, mutual support, and a seeing of our shared humanity.

Key Takeaways

- Beauty becomes an echo of the Divine, allowing us to feel all our feelings and expand our hearts.
- The soul's feelings and the middle senses serve as bridges between our inner experience and the outer world.
- When our feelings are nurtured in this middle phase, new capacities emerge. By awakening to emotions and moving into the world with feeling, we develop in accordance with the natural law of our growth.
- The more adults model compassion and non-judgement, the freer children are to express their feelings, share their experiences, and learn to love others.

Connection & Emotional Needs (7–14 Years)

During these heart-centred years, a child's developmental needs include:

- love for the beauty of the world—experiencing the wonder and awe of life, nature, and art;
- warm enthusiasm for learning—natural curiosity about the world encouraged by loving support and connection;
- a sense of belonging and connection—feeling seen, understood, and accepted by those around them;
- deep feelings of being received and understood—emotional support where their feelings are acknowledged and validated;

- artistic and creative expression—opportunities to express themselves through creativity, developing their individuality; and

- recognition of their unique way of seeing the world—validation of their feelings and perspectives as valuable.

Impact of Unmet Needs

When these soul needs are not met—when a child's feelings are dismissed, when beauty and creativity are not nurtured, or when their unique perspective is overlooked—they may carry a profound longing into adulthood, resulting in:

- a constant need for external validation to feel valued and seen;

- difficulty expressing emotions or processing feelings in a healthy way due to a lack of emotional support;

- struggling to find joy or appreciate life's simple beauties, as they were never taught to recognise or cherish them;

- feeling disconnected from their sense of self, leading to a fragile identity dependent on others' approval; and

- a tendency to suppress their creativity, unable to fully express or recognise their unique perspective.

Healing Meditation

I am inviting you to listen to a meditation I created for you to help heal these heart wounds of lack of feeling and connection. Through these words, you will hear the validation and recognition your soul has been yearning to receive. Let your feelings be held in the gentle embrace of understanding as we restore your capacity for joy and authentic expression of your feeling life.

Beauty in the Soul: A Healing Meditation

Breathe deeply, and allow your awareness to settle into your heart space. These words are for the one within who longed to be truly seen, heard, and cherished in the fullness of their feelings.

Dear Heart, in this sacred pause, feel the gentle awakening of your soul's natural beauty.

The love you sought was always your birthright: unconditional, steady, and true.

Your feelings, in all their depth and richness, are precious treasures.

Each emotion that flows through you is worthy of honour.

The child in you who longed for authentic connection and understanding is being witnessed now.

Feel the warmth blossoming in your heart centre; this is the beauty that has always lived within you, waiting to be recognized.

Your unique way of seeing the world, your creative spirit, your capacity for wonder—these were never meant to be dimmed.

You were always worthy of being delighted in, of having your inner world received with genuine interest.

The conditional love that may have shaped your past does not define your essence or your future creations.

Your heart holds the beauty of a thousand sunsets, the wonder of every star, every flower, every meadow and seashore.

This radiance cannot be diminished by any judgement or misunderstanding. It simply is, as you simply are: complete, beautiful, whole.

Carry this beauty forward, for it is the truth of who you've always been and always will be.

Rest in this space. There is nothing for you to do but be at ease, surrendering to this moment, flowing with each movement and thought.

As these middle years of childhood draw to a close, the emotional capacities formed during this time, along with the foundations of our bodily senses, have laid the groundwork. Our consciousness now moves upward toward the head with focus on the mind and the ability to think independently. We start to seek and question our own unique path and purpose.

In Part Three, we will open another doorway to discover how the spiritually aware mind emerges from the preparation of the feeling life of the middle phase.

Just as we learned that true independence doesn't grow from isolation but from supported connection, we now discover that authentic thinking develops not from intellect alone but from a heart made wise through relationship and engagement with the natural world. We are now going to look at the connection of the heart with the mind, the importance of this stage for the powerful capacity of the mind that begins to create and be in service to inner wisdom built up from the previous two stages.

PART
THREE

GOODNESS IN THE SPIRIT
AGES 14–21

"You may give them your love but not your thoughts,
For they have their own thoughts.
You may house their bodies but not their souls,
For their souls dwell in the house of tomorrow, which you
cannot visit, not even in your dreams."

~ Kahlil Gibran's "On Children" from *The Prophet*

Higher Senses Focus: Listening, Speaking, Thinking, and Sense of *I* (for understanding another *I*—further explored in Chapter 12)

The Learning Journey Stages: Imagination, Innovation to Inspiration

Adult Role/Teen Needs: The Guide

The Guide is a steady, respectful presence that honours inner freedom whilst providing a grounding support. The Guide is a calm and consistent presence who is there to help the teen navigate their emerging independence while staying connected to their values, helping them build a foundation for self-discipline that arises from within rather than being imposed externally.

The Guide offers structure through clear yet flexible boundaries, allowing older children to take increasing responsibility for their choices. For adolescents, the Guide plays a crucial role in balancing support with independence.

This stage is about developing inner freedom within a safe structure, allowing the young adult to explore their identity, ideas, and dreams while knowing they have a trusted presence to turn to. The Guide listens deeply, asks meaningful questions, and provides perspective without imposing rigid control.

Rather than correcting with authority, we can invite reflection, helping adolescents gain confidence in their ability to make wise choices and express themselves fully with hope for the future. This approach empowers and receives the expression of bold and creative ideas with hope for the future.

Payne describes the role as a "companioning authority": someone who listens deeply, asks guiding questions, and models emotional regulation.

CHAPTER 11

THE AWAKENING
MIND AND SPIRIT

WHO WANTS TO HEAR YOUR OPINION?

I feel a passion rise up. I am 16 years old. There is something I want to share, like bubbles coming to the surface of an ever-expanding lake, waiting to be released. My voice feels strong and direct. It comes from the heart of my feelings—the feelings of a young mind about to embark on a journey of discovery in the wider world, outside the home.

Ready to Fly?

I am standing at the doorway
On the threshold of the room
Joining in a conversation ,
Practicing, trusting, experimenting,
Exploring all the changing ideas.
"This is what I think, this is what I feel."

Today
I come in closer, eager to share,
An effervescent energy
Expecting interested listeners.
And then,
An abrupt interruption.
Displeasure, disapproval.
"That's enough, not so loud.
We don't need to hear your opinion
No one is interested in your opinion.
Just who do you think you are,
At your age?
You have far too much to say."
Shame and shock, I stand rigid,
Locked in the body.
Now the inner critical voice speaks back to me.
It is warning me off.
"This is conceited behaviour, not acceptable, you are so
opinionated."
I want to object; indignation arises,
in battle with the inner voice:
"Speak up for yourself!"
But the words are tight in my throat.
My voice becomes weak,
humiliation sets in.
Keep your "ridiculous" passion within.
Stay acceptable.
Follow the rules, fit the mold,

keep the peace.
And then rising up,
soon after the humiliation and the shame,
A new quiet yet rebellious flame.
It begins to magnify in the thoughts of the mind,
A slow burning, a quiet but sacred rage.
Be patient, you can do it.
No need to share so freely with others.
Wait for the day, go it alone.
They don't know what's coming!

Just like the bird who learns to balance between the ground and the sky before its first flight, this new adolescent soul must learn to find a balance between the risk and the challenge—to remain in, or return to, the safety of the nest.

I remember in this instance how my throat closed, swelling as it became an overfull container of ideas, too afraid to be expressed in openness for fear of ridicule or disdain.

Where are the words now buried?

THE AWAKENING OF INDIVIDUAL CONSCIOUSNESS

As we enter the final stage of childhood, a profound shift occurs. The capacity to think for ourselves begins to crystallize, and with it comes the birth of the individual spirit within us. This is not just intellectual growth but an awakening in our minds of the presence of our own spirit.

Our doing, feeling, and thinking capacities—developed through the previous childhood stages—now provide the scaffolding for clarity of thought. Each capacity builds upon the other, flowing together to engage us fully in life. The wisdom of the body, the depth of feeling, and the imagination in the heart all contribute to our highest capacities for thinking, connecting us to insight and inspiration.

This new awakening of individuality yearns to be shared and spoken into life. Our analytical thinking sharpens as we begin to shape a sense of who we are, who we are becoming, and how we relate to others. Our minds become alive with questions, curiosity, and the desire to make sense of the world.

We move beyond simply understanding what things are and how they work to questioning why things are the way they are. It is our nature to change our minds during this phase; changing your mind is helpful, it is growth. Yet, the question arises: Will I be ridiculed for changing my mind?

Adolescents stand at a unique threshold between childhood and adulthood, requiring both steady support and the independence to explore. Here we encounter one of life's greatest mysteries: how each person discovers their unique voice that wants to be shared with the world.

THE QUEST FOR IDENTITY AND VOICE

During this third phase, we embark on a search for meaning and selfhood. The questions that define this time shape the adult we will ultimately become:

What is the right thing?
What do I want from life?
What can I offer? Do I have anything to offer?
What needs to be done for the future?
Who am I?
What do I bring that has value?

How do we honour our individuality, our unique voice, while remaining open to the wisdom of others? How do we stand firm in our convictions while staying flexible enough to grow and change?

When we are not heard or received in the expression of our independent thought, something essential is lost. Without being seen, acknowledged, and valued in our views, we struggle to develop a sense of what we truly think and believe. We may come to rely too heavily on others for our opinions, or we may become rigid and cling to our ideas with a desperate need to be "right"—a need that often masks a deeper longing to feel accepted.

When our relationships become dominated by the need to be right or the fear of being wrong, we lose the ability to let ideas flow freely. The need to have the final say blocks new learning, new possibilities, and new hope in our connections with others.

This is the time when we begin to claim our power as free thinkers, to wonder about divine connection, to break down beliefs, and to experiment with a sense of purpose. It is a time of questioning, testing boundaries, and seeking what truth means while learning to remain open—owning our truth while respecting and honouring the truths of others.

GOODNESS AS THE GUIDING PRINCIPLE

During adolescence and young adulthood, the theme of goodness as a partner of truth becomes the focus. Goodness is not about being perfect or always knowing the right answer. It is characterized by learning how to give of ourselves for what we sense as truth in our body, allowing it to move, to release, to open space—often in tremendous fluctuation—to reconnect to what feels right for the world. Questions about what goodness truly means become crucial:

What do I believe? I do not yet know.
Can I keep working to unravel the ethical dilemmas, seeking what is just and right?
Do I have yet a sense of freedom, or do I have to fight for it?

It is a time to test the waters, experimenting with the art of debating, trying to work out what it means to live a life aligned with deeply held values. It's the phase of discovery, purification, and alignment where the path to our truth begins to take shape.

The thinking mind must first develop its capacities for analysis, questioning, and innovation. The healthy development of these cognitive abilities creates the necessary vessel—a flexible, strong thinking tool capable of receiving something greater.

What we often miss in our intellectual culture is that this development of the thinking mind is not the end point but a preparation. The well-formed intellect becomes, in adulthood beyond age 21, a receptive instrument for inspiration; the mind is refined so that wisdom beyond our personal thinking can flow. Like a musical instrument that must first be properly constructed before it can produce music, the thinking mind must be developed before it can receive and express the higher insights available to human consciousness.

Goodness allows us to share our gifts while receiving the gifts of others. It helps us discern and choose love over fear, openness over defensiveness. It teaches us how to stand in our truth while remaining open to the truth of others, uniting us on a deeper, more empathetic level.

THE ROLE OF THE ADULT GUIDE

For adolescents to flourish, they need to feel safe and connected within their family unit, supported by adults who express *interest* in their growth rather than trying to control it. They need adults who can guide rather than overprotect, allowing them to express their natural curiosity and ask all the questions they need to ask.

This Guide points toward possible directions for the future while allowing the adolescent's changing opinions to be held and released with flexibility.

Peers going through the same stages can be helpful, but they cannot substitute for the Guide—a human who has lived a little more, who has traveled further on their own path. When connection with trusted adults is lacking, we can feel uncertain and very lost in our sense of direction at this time in our lives.

The core being of the parent or teacher as Guide focuses on keeping alive hope for the future and pointing to possibility. The adult Guide acts according to intuition and trusts in the adolescent's unique journey, rather than projecting their own dreams or longings. They see who this human being is really becoming, asking inwardly, How can I help this teen on their journey?

This involves truthful, authentic sharing to maintain trust and hope—even when it's difficult for parents who may have great fear and anxiety during this stage their child is in. Adults often foresee outcomes and predict challenges and failure, yet it is also a great learning opportunity to let go where the danger is not life-threatening.

To be listened to openly, with interest and without criticism, is our deepest wish. At this time in life, when we begin to discover the reasons for our being as our passions and interests grow in our hearts, we learn more about who we are.

We need the ones within our families, at school, and in college who we trust to have our back—the ones we deeply need to see and acknowledge us, however wild and ridiculous our ideas may seem. These ideas, which adults might dismiss as unrealistic, actually fuel hope and passion for life.

As the Guides, we want to keep communication open so young people feel safely held while remaining open to guidance. Our guidance should feel loving, not stifling. Our interest in their ideas must be enthusiastic, ongoing, and alive.

If in early childhood the world was perceived as good and beautiful, then the wisdom of what is always possible remains within. The unfolding of the previous stages allows for the hope and creative thought to send us forth like the arrows in Gibran's poem: "You are the bows from which your children as living arrows are sent forth."

THE HEALING POWER OF RETURNING TO REVERENT CARE

When an adolescent has shut down—when it has become hard for them to share openly—the adult can return to supporting safety in the body. We begin in small and simple ways that may seem insignificant but carry a powerful impact.

With quiet and loving intention, we can reverently care for our adolescent child's belongings, as we did when we nurtured the body of the small child. This reverent care is not merely tidying up; it is approaching their possessions with a deep respect that acknowledges the sacred nature of what belongs to them. When we handle their books, their clothing, their treasured objects with genuine care and attention, we create a powerful energetic shift that the adolescent can feel, even if nothing is spoken

This simple act of reverent attention creates a sense of more ease and openness in the body. It is a wordless communication that says, "I respect your boundaries. I honour your space. I see the value in what matters to you." This reverence extends beyond physical objects to include respect for their ideas, their privacy, and their emerging selfhood.

We can also create safety at mealtimes, where nourishment becomes a ritual of care rather than a functional necessity. For with well-being in the body, feelings once again are freed and strength for clarity of their thinking is restored. These practices become nourishing, too, for the adult in the process.

I discovered this during evening meal preparations in our home. The kitchen became a naturally safe space for connection with my teenage boys—warm, filled with inviting aromas, and beautifully non-confrontational. While my hands were busy chopping vegetables or stirring pots, they would often drift in and casually bring up things that were bothering them. These spontaneous conversations proved far more fruitful than any "we need to talk" moments in bedrooms or formal sitting areas. There was something about the side-by-side nature of kitchen work, where I wasn't solely focussed on extracting information, that allowed them to feel less scrutinized and more comfortable sharing their thoughts. The kitchen's sensory richness—warmth, scent, taste—combined with purposeful activity created a container where difficult topics could emerge naturally, without pressure.

This reverent care creates an environment where the adolescent can feel seen without being invaded, respected without being abandoned, and supported without being controlled. It represents a profound understanding that the way we handle the physical world reflects and impacts the inner emotional world. Such care becomes a form of meditation in action, teaching through example rather than instruction.

As the adult shifts from controlling to reverently caring, the adolescent's natural defenses can begin to soften. Trust can gradually rebuild, creating openings for authentic connection that no amount of questioning or demanding could achieve. This reverent attitude toward their belongings, their space, and ultimately their being becomes a communication of reverence that speaks directly to their soul.

"Looking deeply at any one thing
We see the whole cosmos
The one is made of the many
To take care of ourselves,
We take care of those around us."

~ Thich Nhat Hanh, various teachings.

THE HIGHER SENSES IN ACTION

We have a sense of hearing. A sound occurs and enters our ears, where we process it and develop an understanding. The sound is transformed into meaning, and we hear speech. The gifts of the senses of speaking, listening, and thinking are like portals—tools for ultimately receiving divine inspiration when we become attuned, when we bring in presence, when we quiet distractions and become still. We need to be still to really *hear*.

In speaking, we need the voice that expresses what calls to be shared. Ideas arise in our hearts, are processed in our minds, and then yearn to be shared—as written words or in conversation or speech. Without a receiver, words seem to fall into emptiness, forgotten and dissolved. Our expression feels most delightful when we picture the one who will receive it, who might be nourished by our sharing, allowing the connection of understanding to fill us both.

Our human experience requires that we develop a sense of self so we can freely choose moments to put aside our self-contained thoughts and open space for others because we genuinely want to understand. We want to know the free thoughts of others, not because we should but because we feel the power of freedom that is innately ours and present in the other. Our choice is where it begins. Love is not love when it is unfree.

Our gifts for connection—listening, speaking, and thinking—help us cross the bridge into another's experience. Throughout the teenage years and into the early twenties, we need an effective thinking partner whose listening ignites thinking rather than just preparation of a clever reply.

A listener and speaker create energy together. When I speak and am received with interest, it creates movement and aliveness, revealing who I am. Having my voice heard helps me stand strong and gives me roots. When I am deeply listened to, I feel what it's like to be *heard*, and I become a better listener for others.

When we can share our waiting expressions in spaces where we are allowed to be fully ourselves, we come closer to the "real me" version of ourselves. This is the gift of the liberated senses of speech and listening.

Key Takeaways

- Inner freedom fuels confidence: Adolescents develop confidence when they are given the freedom to think independently, make choices, and take responsibility for their actions. Without this, they may struggle to trust themselves and will rely too heavily on external validation.

- Signs of suppressed inner freedom: When a young person's thoughts, opinions, or desires are dismissed, their ability to think independently weakens, leading to lack of self-trust, dependency on others, and fear of being wrong.

- The role of the adult shifts now from Gardener of the child's gifts to Guide for their emerging selfhood. This Guide points toward possible directions for the future while allowing the adolescent's changing opinions to be held and released with flexibility.

- To be listened to openly, with interest and without criticism, is the adolescent's deepest wish. At this time in life, when we begin to discover the reasons for our being as our passions and interests grow in our hearts, we learn more about who we are.

Inner Freedom Needs (14–21 Years)

To develop into confident, self-assured adults, adolescents require:

- hope for the future—belief that their ideas and efforts can lead to meaningful outcomes;

- self-confidence in thinking and speaking—the ability to express their ideas without fear;

- freedom to explore new ideas—encouragement to question, experiment, and discover;

- respect for their viewpoints—knowing their opinions are heard and valued;

- support for emerging ideals—guidance as they form their own beliefs and values; and

- trust in their ability to decide—opportunities to make choices and learn from them

Impact of Unmet Needs

When these needs go unmet—when a young person's thoughts are dismissed, their ideals mocked, or their voice silenced—they may enter adulthood without trust in their own wisdom. This can result in:

- dependence on external validation—always seeking approval instead of trusting themselves;
- rigid thinking—fear of uncertainty leading to inflexible beliefs and resistance to growth;
- fear of speaking their truth—hesitancy to share authentic thoughts and feelings;
- difficulty connecting to purpose—struggling to identify and pursue meaningful goals; and
- rebellious behaviour or excessive conformity—either rejecting or over-identifying with external authority.

Practices for Adults

- Active listening *without* blame, criticism, or uncalled for advice
- Validation of emerging perspectives
- Encouragement of independent thinking

Remember that your body will know the TRUTH. When you are stuck in your thinking, disconnected from your feelings, go back to the previous stages to see if you can glimpse what you might be longing for.

GOODNESS IN THE SPIRIT: A HEALING MEDITATION

I am inviting you to listen to a meditation I created for you to help heal these wounds of speaking and listening from your truest self. Let your unique way of seeing the world be honoured as we restore your trust in your own knowing and your freedom to think independently.

Take a full, deep breath and feel yourself fully present. Become conscious of the sensations in the body. There is nothing you need to do or change. These words speak to the *part of you that longed for freedom to discover your own truth and voice.*

In this moment of stillness, recognize the sacred flame of your unique consciousness.

The inner freedom you sought was always your divine inheritance; to think, to question, to discover your own path is part of the design. All will bring you back to a place of ease and presence, to the wellspring of your soul.

Your voice matters. Your thoughts are worthy of expression. The adolescent self who yearned to be heard, to have ideas received with respect and interest, is being honoured now.

Feel the clarity and light arising within your mind.

This is the goodness that has always guided you, even when external voices attempted to silence your wisdom. Your perspective, your questions, your emerging sense of purpose—these were always meant to be celebrated.

You were always worthy of being trusted with your own becoming.

The judgement or dismissal that may have clouded your confidence does not limit the brilliance of your inner knowing.

Your spirit holds a purpose that only you can fulfill, a goodness that seeks expression through your unique gifts.

This inner guidance cannot be diminished by doubt or fear. It simply awaits your recognition.

You are free to think, to create, to become.

This freedom is the essence of your spirit, now and always.

As the child moves toward adolescence, the foundation laid in these middle years becomes crucial. When young voices are silenced or withdrawn, their emerging thoughts and creative expressions may become trapped within. The path to restoring confidence lies in what we've explored throughout this section—creating environments of safety and trust where feelings can surface naturally. This sacred holding of space, which we'll explore more deeply in the next chapter, allows the unfolding mind to reconnect with its innate wisdom and find its authentic voice in the world.

In the next chapter, "Sacred Listening Practice," we'll explore how deep, empathetic listening can heal and nurture this process. Just as the body needs care to restore well-being, the soul requires attentive listening to grow as the spirit is received and wisdom is heard. Listening, witnessing—not to fix or judge but to be present and open to another's unfolding inner world—offers the very connection that adolescents long for. Through this sacred form of listening, trust is rebuilt and the space for independent thinking and emotional expression can be reclaimed.

CHAPTER 12

SACRED LISTENING PRACTICE

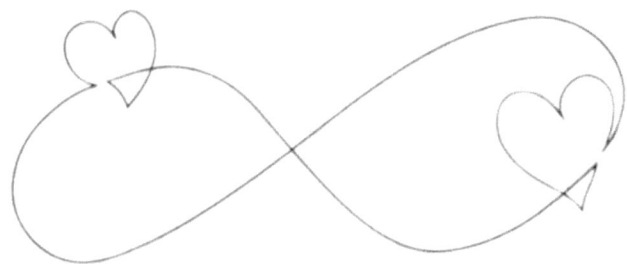

"The Soul has been given its own ears, to hear the things the mind does not understand."

~ Rumi

To listen deeply is a gift for both the listener and the speaker, for in learning to listen from my wholeness, I hear so much more, taking in all that my ears alone cannot reveal to me.

Deep, empathetic listening is what we all truly want. The connection to another person—someone who listens powerfully, without judgement, without hidden control—is the healing safe space that we instinctively seek. We long to be held with all that arises in thoughts and feelings as they come.

We come together to express and not impress. What a beautiful relief!

THE ART OF SACRED LISTENING

The Chinese character for listening reveals an ancient wisdom. It is built of five intricate elements: ears, eyes, heart, "one," and "king." Each component reveals a deeper dimension of what true listening entails.

The first three elements are intuitive: listening involves hearing with your ears, observing clearly with your eyes (as though you had ten eyes!), and connecting with your heart. Hearing captures sound, seeing captures gesture and micro-movement, and feeling captures emotions.

The other two elements offer subtle yet powerful insights. The line representing "one" symbolises undivided attention, an unwavering focus on the speaker. It demands attention, deepening into presence to allow the speaker to say freely whatever needs to be said.

The element "king" introduces a regal dimension, suggesting listening at its most noble and elevated form. Here, it means not just royalty but excellence—the highest, most refined practice of the art of listening. We can link this king element to the sense of "*I*"—the "I am" that transcends the material world, the likes and dislikes, the grievances of the mind. It is the part of oneself linked with inspiration and insight from the place where we are able to understand another, and to see the "*I*" of the other. Essentially, the king or queen is the true "*I*"—our true sovereign being—that chooses to let go for the sake of the other.

When all the elements are combined, this Chinese character communicates a profound truth: the most exceptional listening is a holistic experience that embraces bodily awareness, emotional intelligence, and absolute focussed attention—a complete and sovereign presence for the one speaking.

OUR JOURNEY WITH LISTENING

I want to share a revolutionary listening practice that will help you develop more trust in speaking your innermost thoughts and bring you an opportunity to be heard in a way that goes far beyond any kind of listening technique you have ever experienced.

In times of feeling disconnected, our challenges often stem from disagreements over what is true. We think we are "truth seekers," yet we find it so hard to see the truth expressed differently from our own felt sense of truth. We have default reactions. We fall in and out of relationships depending on whether we like or dislike, agree or disagree with the words or behaviour of the other. Our expectation of the other conforming to *our* way of seeing the world becomes the thickest of barriers to our understanding.

We have come to see through the phases of childhood that our preoccupation with being right comes from not being *really* heard, especially in the teen years. When we fight to be right, to defend our sense of self, we see the other as wrong and believe they need correcting. Or, we assume we know the other's intentions, and we quickly make a judgement. This is automatic and remains unconscious as we continue to avoid it out of programmed fear. We will deny it. We think we are good listeners.

What is actually happening is that from our place of fear we say inwardly, *I know what you think because I have already put you in a box. You are out to get me.*

We do not realise we are unconsciously demanding, so we move further away from the healing place of true connection. We play out our unmet needs and discover our own blocks as we practice listening.

Perhaps we make the outer appearance of listening for a while, yet all the time we are waiting to give advice so that others will agree with us. We will keep the peace when they obey. If they choose a different path, we will be threatened, for they no longer respect us.

THE PRACTICE OF SACRED LISTENING

Would you like to rediscover listening? We can take listening—to ourselves, to each other, to our children, and to the voice within—to another level. We listen with our twelve senses; we listen with body, heart, and mind so we can receive from the spirit. It is the pathway to the greatest wisdom.

In practice with a listening partner, we can experience sitting through the pauses that once seemed so uncomfortable and discover fullness instead of emptiness.

You will come to realise that you have deeply held questions and wishes:

What do I think?
Help me discover what I think.
I want to know what I feel.
I want to allow whatever needs to be expressed without any fear of judgement.
Who am I really?
I need time to explore and discover myself for myself.
What is for the good?
I need to work it out so I feel it in my body.
It feels so strange, as we are sitting in the gaps,
Those pauses cease to be awkward.
No need to fill them right now.
I can rest in it; you can be present.
Those pauses become pregnant with wisdom.
Please just listen, to hear what will be birthed.

And so we learn to listen.

I promise to learn to listen better every day.
I come from my strong inner presence.
I choose to direct my attention to you.

I listen so you can hear yourself speak, and you are heard
so you understand so much more and so much better.
I am able to step into your world and understand
("understand" literally means "to stand under another").
I free you to discover your authentic self, and in that liberation, you
can truly hear yourself.
I can bear with you, in our shared humanity---not take away, not
distract and divert, but allow, and be with you.

We need listeners who stand strong in their own energy, who do not fall asleep into our words passive and agreeing but instead are fully present, awake, and inwardly active. We need the listener who brings their whole self, a listener who does not listen for what they can gain, does not listen out of obedience but from their ability to see us with a deep wish to help us know what we think, to know more of who we are.

And in their warm focussed interest, they, too, are blessed with new insights, and all that is expressed is transformed in the space between us.

LISTENING WITH AND FOR CHILDREN

We can learn to listen with an open heart, as we once did in the innocent wisdom of childhood. As little children, we were fine-tuned to take everything in; we did not discriminate. We resonated in devotion. This is where we can learn from children now.

However, as children in our emerging being, we were not designed or yet ready to analyse or hold focussed space for others, as we were still forming the foundations we needed for our own growth, our own evolving awareness.

As children, we acted on what called us from within, guided unconsciously by innate intuition for what we needed to learn and grow. For our task was to form ourselves after the role models of the adults. We observed everything. When overwhelmed, we filtered what we could, but we did not take it in intellectually; we were not ready for rational explanations.

"You are not listening!"

How often do children say this to parents? We also say this to our children and our partners. We may have learnt that to "listen" means to comply, obey or agree with.

When we speak too long and explain too much to children, telling them they must listen and complaining when they do not, we have become diverted away from our own ability to understand what is needed in the moment. We want to get a point across. We overexplain in the hope they will somehow get it. We speak so they will obey us, and we mistake obedience for "listening."

To listen means to be still, and yet little children are continually on the move. They are born to move. When we force them to listen, we actually program them to tune us out. The hands over the ears are the sign that it's all too much!

Listening then becomes something to dread in the future, a hindrance, and we cannot shake off the programmed response, even when as adults we try so hard to be "good" listeners. And yet we sense the, "You are not listening. You never listen!"

For children, especially those under age 7, deeper communication happens unconsciously through the body and behaviour and not so much through words. Listening to children from our adult self is also attentive observation (see the child study in Chapter 3).

THE TRANSFORMATIVE POWER OF LISTENING

When we can hear ourselves speak completely uninterrupted, we are surprised, as if for the first time, with what appears. It is as though speech speaks *through* us, and at last we hear from beyond our limited mind.

Profound invitations emerge. We did not realise how large, wide, and wise our inspirations could be! When we move into deep listening, our communication moves beyond all the words and becomes a sacred communion.

As adults, we listen to another as they speak their truth. When it is our turn, we also hear ourselves speak out what feels true to us. In this reciprocal act of intentional connection, in full attention for our speaking and listening, both partners expand into the fullness of the human experience, held in our bodies with compassion, in the hearts of each other.

With our offering—with our opening of compassion—light of true knowing can enter; it's a light that cleanses and shines a brighter light for everyone. Old stuck beliefs are washed away. The loving and real truth of our being is now revealed.

A listener in the strength of their true "*I*" becomes the source of the true reflection of what we wanted to say. They become the container for us to go forward in a shared strength. They give us the courage to find out more of what we need to know.

Each time afresh, we can practice holding faith for the inner wisdom within each person. We can learn to breathe into the fullness of the silence where our deepest intuitions live: intuitions revealed as gifts for us both, insights that ignite us to the right action with a passion that calls us to share, without hesitation, for the well-being of others.

As we hold ourselves grounded in our body for those we listen to, we allow them to courageously take their next step. We listen because it is an act of love.

The highest form of the sense of ego, or individuality, is not defined by how loudly we express ourselves but by how deeply we choose to connect with and understand others. When we choose to bridge the gap between our individuality and our shared humanity, we create the possibility for something greater than ourselves: a life rooted in love and goodness.

When we truly open to listen in group discussions, we can tap into a deeper well of shared understanding. This allows us to make the best choices, moving beyond the narrow views that divide us. By being fully present and open to each other's perspectives, we uncover insights that go beyond our individual opinions or biases. This collective wisdom is the key to unlocking solutions that serve us all.

Wouldn't you like to be in that space?

Would you love to give that to another?

It is through the energy of those who see and accept us as we are, who really want to know what we think and will wait until we finish speaking, that we have the power to speak our greatest potential into life. There is a magical and spiritual element to deep listening, a limitless flow of wisdom that is created between us:

When I keep coming back to recognise my whole self, I release space to receive what you say, and so we are both freed.

I am passionate about the power of real listening. I know how it opens doorways to so much more understanding. Listening is an expression of love that transcends separation, where our shared beings merge as we hold and appreciate all apparent differences. This kind of listening capacity is enabled in the healing of our childhood wounds.

You are here to listen to your children, your partners, and old friends and new.

Are you ready to be blessed with the greatest insights as you listen in the way you are designed to do, to remember who you are?

AUTHENTIC PRESENCE IN LISTENING

To be faithful to authentic listening means staying true to yourself in your listening for the other.

You do not have to agree.

You do not listen to be "good" or to please.

You do not listen out of fear but out of your decision to love.

FOR LOVE IS A DECISION.

When you cannot listen any longer, you stay close to your truth. You speak it with love, you take a break, you take the time you need, and you return when you are ready.

YOUR COURAGE FOR THE TRUTH SETS YOU BOTH FREE.

Perhaps thinking about all these parts whilst listening may feel overwhelming.

To help calm the overwhelm, I share a listening practice that is a deliberate, gentle, self-paced discovery of body, soul, and spirit. I invite you to join me in one of my live workshops where we will break down the parts in a simple four-step process through body, heart, mind, and spirit (QR code found below).

This kind of listening is accessible to us all, and we can practice any time we find ourselves listening. It is a return to wholeness and freedom as we release the obstacles that seem to get in the way and block our ability to hear more deeply what is being said.

We all need a space where we can release, reveal, and safely be held just as we are. We need this space to just *be* so we can unlock our hearts. Below is the link if you want to find out more about the listening practice to transform your relationships and your connection to yourself.

Learn to listen, and free yourself.

Let your unique way of seeing the world be honoured as we restore your trust in your own knowing and your freedom to think independently.

This most beautiful poem below seems to capture the essence of my experience into the mystery of presence, attention, and connection summed up in the practice of listening deeply within, listening to the world around us and bringing loving attention to hear another:

> *Awaken to the mystery of being here and enter the quiet immensity of your own presence.*
> *Have joy and peace in the temple of your senses.*
> *Receive encouragement when new frontiers beckon.*
> *Respond to the call of your gift and the courage to follow its path.*
> *Let the flame of anger free you of all falsity.*
> *May warmth of heart keep your presence aflame.*
> *May anxiety never linger about you.*
> *May your outer dignity mirror an inner dignity of soul.*
> *Take time to celebrate the quiet miracles that seek no attention.*
> *Be consoled in the secret symmetry of your soul.*
> *May you experience each day as a sacred gift woven around the heart of wonder.*
>
> **~ John O'Donohue, "For Presence," from *To Bless the Space Between Us: A Book of Blessings***

As we conclude our brief exploration of sacred listening (there is so much more to discover!) we find ourselves naturally returning to where our journey began. We've travelled through the landscapes of childhood development: the body's truth, the heart's beauty, and the mind's capacity for goodness.

Like water flowing in a spiral, moving outward only to return to its source, we now circle back to our starting point with deeper insight and more spacious presence. The sanctuary awaits our return, eternally unchanged in its essence, yet we approach it now from a deeper place within ourselves, able to see more, receive more, and bring more of our authentic being to each other.

INTEGRATION OF WISDOM:
A PERSONAL JOURNEY

There are moments in our lives that seem to mirror each other across time, offering us the chance to see how we've changed. For me, these bookends of transformation appeared in the two scenes I described in Chapter 1: first as a young mother at a nursery school doorway, and later as a grandmother by a hospital incubator.

In that first moment at the nursery school, my throat closed tight as the teacher instructed me to leave quickly, despite my daughter's tears. Though my body signaled distress—shallow breathing, racing heart, a heavy weight in my stomach—I couldn't translate these sensations into words or action. My heart ached with uncertainty, yet I remained silent. The disconnect between what I sensed in my body, felt in my heart, and could not unravel with my mind left me frozen, unable to speak my truth.

This silence wasn't from lack of care but from a fragmentation within myself. My thinking mind had become separated from the wisdom of my body and the intuitive feelings of my heart. The words I needed remained trapped inside, unformed and inaccessible.

Years later, standing by my grandson's incubator, with the nurse who told me I shouldn't stay long, it felt different. I felt the same initial flutter of anxiety, but instead of disconnection, something remarkable happened, an experience of a feeling of wholeness, a strength, an integration and an alignment: the truth sensed by my body, the love flowing through my heart, and the clarity of my thinking mind coming together as one in quiet harmony.

The words came not from defiance or fear but from a centred place where all aspects of my being seemed to work together. My response wasn't loud or confrontational—it was simply clear, grounded, and true.

I've come to understand a personal truth about aligned connection to the quiet space of presence, as Mary Anne Radmacher so beautifully expressed in her book *Courage Doesn't Always Roar*: My journey between these two moments wasn't really about becoming more forceful or outspoken but about patiently reintegrating the wisdom of body, heart, and mind until they could work together as one.

THE SACRED POWER OF BEING HEARD

What made this integration possible? Beyond my own inner work, there was something equally transformative: the experience of being truly listened to. In the years between these two moments, I discovered what it means to be heard at the deepest level—not just my words but my whole being.

Through my own implementation of the listening practices I described in Chapter 12, I found companions who could hold space without judgement, who could bear witness to my slow attempts to express what I barely understood myself. In the sacred container of their attention, my fragmented self began to find wholeness again.

When someone listens to us with their entire being— free of quick advice, in body, heart, and mind fully present—something miraculous happens: The words we couldn't form before begin to take shape. The knowing that lived in our bodies but couldn't reach our conscious minds finds its way into language. The emotions that churned chaotically begin to arrange themselves into meaningful patterns.

Being listened to so we can hear our truth creates the conditions for our own inner listening to deepen. As others held space for me without trying to fix or change my experience, I learned to stay present with all parts of myself: the uncomfortable sensations, the difficult emotions, the contradictory thoughts. And through the practice of returning to presence, thoughts and sensations gradually wove together the strands of wisdom that had been separated.

This integration doesn't happen overnight. It unfolds gradually through countless small acts of reconnection, moments when we pause to feel what our bodies are sensing, when we honour the truth of our emotions, when we allow our thoughts to arise from this solid foundation rather than from fear or conditioning.

ALWAYS UNFOLDING

I want to be clear—I'm not sharing this as someone who has "arrived" at some perfect state of integration . . . far from it! My journey continues every day with moments of beautiful connection followed by times when I stumble back into old patterns. There are still days when my throat tightens, when my body's wisdom gets muffled by mental noise, when I miss opportunities to speak truth with love.

And I've come to see that each person's path toward wholeness looks different. What awakened integration for me may not be what you need. The window through which wisdom reveals itself opens differently for each of us. Some find their way through creative expression, others through movement, stillness, nature, or relationship. There is no single correct path—only the one that resonates with your unique being.

What matters isn't perfection but the willingness to remain open—to hold our experiences with compassion, to listen to what they're trying to teach us, and to allow our awareness to expand. This ongoing process has shown me how much richer life becomes when we're willing to be both a perfectly imperfect human and a vessel for something greater than ourselves.

What I hope to share through my story and my work is how this wholeness becomes possible. When our embodied truth from childhood grounds us, when our feeling life from the middle years connects us, our thinking capacity becomes not just intellectual but inspired, able to express what needs to be spoken with a quiet strength.

The courage to speak our truth emerges not from forcing ourselves to be bold but from allowing all parts of ourselves to come into alignment.

This is the essence of what I offer in my work now—creating spaces where this kind of deep listening can occur, where fragmented parts can be reunited, where wisdom can flow freely between body, heart, and mind. It is through authentic connection, in warm presence and attention, that our hearts will soften and reconnect to the essence of our being.

HOMECOMING

RETURN TO THE SANCTUARY

The time will come
when, with elation,
you will greet yourself arriving
at your own door, in your own mirror,
and each will smile at the other's welcome.

~ Derek Walcott, "Love after Love"

Let's now take a rest from our wanderings through the phases of childhood to reflect on what has been gathered. We are coming back to our cosy, relaxing space. The teapot has been refilled. The soft light of early evening fills our space with a glow.

We have taken in the power of being held and accepted, back to the source of our first experiences at birth, and we have explored the three phases of childhood—from bodily truth through the heart's beauty to the mind's ability to hear and perceive the light of goodness.

We have looked at what happens to our needs and the longings that emerged when the needs were not met. We have observed the ways we feel lost on our childhood journey and found the blocks that seem to obstruct our experience of flow.

We have uncovered unique stories and seen how we can share, hear, and heal with our true listening and speaking. To be with each other, as we process; we sense this truth in our bodies as our purpose.

What we realise is that in our surrender to what is, in each part of ourselves, our being begins to flow harmoniously as needed for the present moment. The Divine flows in and through us, and we are surrendered to the full expression of our soul.

We say that children grow up, and as spiritual beings, we also grow down into the body. Spiritual essence—that which holds us together—gently begins to descend, gradually infusing our human body and guiding it within for life here on earth. Our spiritual being directs the formation of our body and then begins to wake us up, in perfect timing, into the potential of a full conscious awareness.

In conscious awareness we hear the messages we are longing to hear, honouring individual expression for the purpose of realising love on earth (see Diagram in Appendix 1).

For our spirit in consciousness wakes up in a perfect order, in our human form, from body to soul to mind. What a miracle that a child begins to walk, talk and think, in that wise order, in only the first three years of life!

As adults we bless our children, not with techniques, instructions, and strategies but in our attention, in being fully present, and in being a loving role model.

Take heart and trust that the more presence we practice, the more we allow light to shine through for others, not in perfection but in authenticity and acceptance, as human beings in a process. This is the authenticity that every child, every human being searches for.

Shining a light on the deep, unconscious longings we carry from childhood allows the felt hindrances to be heard more clearly and move within the body. We can listen, yet we do not need to identify. We can allow them; our longings speak to us and show us the way home. We can be grateful for them, like guideposts pointing us back to our true centre.

You do not have to see healing as a long, difficult, or lonely journey, and you do not need to constantly rely on someone you believe has more wisdom than you. The wisdom you seek is already within you, waiting to be recognized. In freedom, we can shift our attention to the stillness of presence, and from there we can release the wisdom waiting for our soul to receive it.

We come to realise that focussing solely on our own individual struggles can create a one-way inward spiral that traps us in a cycle of revisiting old memories that have no outlet, leading to feelings of frustration, hopelessness, and fear.

But, when we choose to set aside the conceptual self, the pressing wants and needs for this moment of connection with each other, we experience an opening and a space. "When I listen to you, *for* you, I come to realise I am also listening to me." There is no difference in the giving and receiving as wisdom speaks in the space we made between us.

In relationship and in connection to all the things of the earth, the way out becomes the restoration of the way back in—it is shown to us in our unique stories—as we speak them out for each other to hold, as we allow them without judgement. This is the healing medicine.

We connect with each other in conscious awareness, and we rest in the strength of still presence. It is a beautiful dance of presence and connection, as in freedom we shift our attention wherever it needs to go.

"The Bell Ringing Verse" by Rudolf Steiner:

> *To wonder at **beauty**,*
> *Stand guard over **truth**,*
> *Look up to the noble,*
> *Resolve on the **good**.*
> *This leadeth us truly*
> *To purpose in living,*
> *To right in our **doing**,*
> *To peace in our feeling,*
> *To light in our **thinking**.*

And teaches us trust,
In the working of God,
In all that there is,
In the width of the world,
In the depth of the soul.

As we now reconnect with the truth, beauty, and goodness that we rediscovered on our journey together, we begin to bring in more presence to our conscious wisdom as parent, grandparent, teacher or friend. And we more readily access daily presence for greater insights that help us bring compassion and healing for our own inner child.

In our reclaiming of presence, we recognise where we are in our own process and can nurture ourselves through the beauty of what we love, connecting to the natural world, experiencing the feeling of abundance and gratitude.

In fully living in this way, we become free to provide children with the nurturing, understanding, and support that we now recognize they require to fully express themselves in each of the three stages.

In loving *them* free of your projections, you will heal and free yourself.

We find ourselves drawn to compassion for our fellow human beings, recognizing that they, too, share our human experience, that we are both human and Divine. In this realization, we now understand— deeply feel the truth—that we are indeed *all in this together*.

Imagine a world grounded in compassion and genuine presence, where we do not exhaust our supply of love but see how it is continually renewed, how it continues to replenish and energise us.

This famous verse by Steiner reflects a beautiful truth of our shared being. It gives us powerful support when we struggle to remember in times of disconnection and conflict:

"Faithfulness"

Let your loyalty to another human being come about in this way: there will be moments—quickly passing by— when he will seem to you filled and illumined by the true, primal image of his spirit.

Then can come, yes, will come, long stretches of time when your fellow-being seems clouded, even darkened. But learn at these times to say to yourself: The spirit will strengthen me; I will remember the true, unchanging image that I once saw. Nothing at all—neither deception nor disguise—can take it away from me.

Struggle again and again for the true picture that you saw. The struggle itself is your faithfulness.

And in those efforts to be faithful and to trust, a human being will come close to another as if with an angel's power of protection.

~ Translated by Hans and Ruth Putsch)

We are the reminders for each other that we are always whole.
Wholeness is our holiness.
We are searching for the one who has faith in us.
You are this person.
You are the gift.
Your presence and your time are your greatest gifts.

A VISION OF A LISTENING SPACE

"Child of God, you were created to create the good, the beautiful, and the holy. Do not forget this."
~ Helen Schucman, *A Course in Miracles*

I have an image of a place, like an offering of time, a sacred sanctuary of authentic reconnection and loving presence.

It is a conscious, sacred listening space. It is the Listening Sanctuary. It can be expressed in the creation of a physical space and a place between hearts.

The oasis I created—Highgate House School—will continue to stand on the Peak for at least another year. And yet, I wonder, what is my work if the physical space of the school ceases to exist?

How do we nurture the being of this beautiful community, how do we feel and know its purpose each day?

How will this work—where people can come to be heard and reconnect to themselves and others with ease, trust, and joy—continue to manifest on this physical earth?

As I ponder these questions, I come to realise that my work is in becoming an Intuitive Guide who will lead those also asking these questions and seeking a community that is a sanctuary for themselves and others to create: create the sanctuaries!

A sanctuary can reach and fill the many layers of our being. This sanctuary emerges like a passion project, a reverent container designed to reawaken inner knowing and authentic connection.

The whole environment and energy created is filled with a simple beauty and the soft embrace of profound acceptance and safety. The listening space for children and for adults is a living vessel for deep relational healing.

Within the "walls" of this space we can rediscover the tender, unguarded essence of the inner child through compassionate remembrance and regenerative connection.

This vision feels as though it is not just *my* dream; it is God's wish, the energy of love implanted in every soul, every person alive on this earth.

This is humanity's shared mission and purpose, to step boldly into our interconnectedness, to nurture the bonds that unite us, and to inspire a legacy of kindness that echoes through generations.

Warmth—like the primordial warmth of life—is generated when we bring all of who we are to another; it has a power far greater than we could ever imagine in our human mind.

Human life begins in warmth.

We pass on the warmth generated in our heart to others so they remember their sacred origin. In turn, warmth is renewed in them, and so it goes on from one to the other with the power to transform wider and farther, from one small movement, one drop, to ripple outward through generations and heal the disconnection felt in the world.

"Love is the water of life. Drink it down with heart and soul."

~ **Rumi**

In free expression of our being, we create a flow that is a wellspring—a clear, unlimited, and vibrant source. We become the vessel that both contains and channels this flow. In the infinite space between our hearts we invite a luminous drop of light, and it is here that true wisdom is heard.

Here in this space, partners, parents, children, and friends, are not being "fixed" but deeply heard and supported in remembering: peace and harmony are revealed as having always been ours, connection and presence are reclaimed, and we find that delicate bridge between us where masks fall away and hearts speak their truth.

This book is not an ending but a beginning.

If you feel drawn to continue this journey in community with others who are walking a similar path, I welcome your connection. The practices and insights we've explored together deepen when shared in companionship with fellow travellers.

I offer small listening circles and guided practices to support you in integrating these insights into your daily life and relationships. These gatherings provide a container where you can be truly heard, where your unique journey is honoured, and where the community's collective wisdom becomes a resource for all.

In this sacred unfolding, we become both container and content, transforming fear into love, empty loneliness into the fullness of interconnected presence. In this recognition, the perceived boundaries between us dissolve: the never ending dance of spirit and matter united in the now.

As we remember and are remembered, as we see and are truly seen, we build the resilient connected communities our world so deeply needs.

APPENDIX 1

A SUMMARY DIAGRAM:
THE INNER WISDOM COMPASS

Inner Wisdom Compass

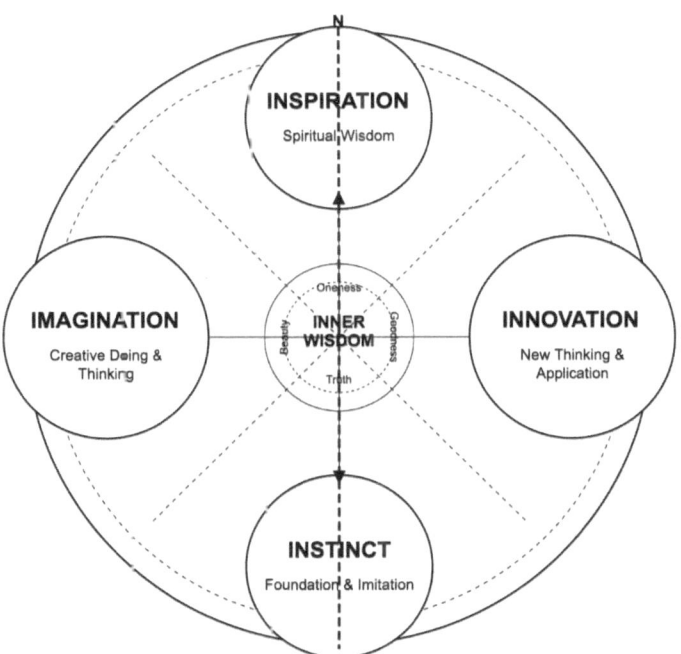

N

INSPIRATION
Spiritual Wisdom

IMAGINATION
Creative Doing & Thinking

Oneness
INNER WISDOM
Beauty · Goodness
Truth

INNOVATION
New Thinking & Application

INSTINCT
Foundation & Imitation

"Our learning journey flows from instinct to imagination to innovation to inspiration."

HEALING PHRASES FOR THE JOURNEY HOME

I offer these healing phrases as touchstones for your continued journey. Each one emerges from deep understanding of what the human heart needs to hear at different stages of development and healing.

These are not just affirmations to be repeated mechanically, adding to your to do list. Rather, they are medicine for the soul, carefully crafted to address the specific longings and needs that arise from our earliest experiences. Whether you find yourself seeking to heal the physical security of early childhood, the emotional connections of the middle years, or the spiritual seeking of adolescence, there is medicine here for you.

Some of these phrases will resonate more strongly than others. Some may even bring up resistance or discomfort—this too is valuable information about where healing is needed. Let them work on you gradually, like gentle rain softening hardened earth.

Use these phrases *as meditation focuses* when you are triggered by old patterns.

To heal specific childhood wounds, these phrases are to help you to remember your essence in difficult moments and to be used as bridges to help you come back to your authentic self.

My hope is that they help you feel seen, supported, and uplifted. Most of all, I want you to know that the message of these meditations is always available to you, no matter where you are in life. You are loved, and you are whole.

Remember, longings are not weakness; they are the voice of wisdom calling us home to wholeness. As we learn to hear and honour them, we begin to heal not just ourselves but all the children, those we are with now and those who live in our memory.

Most importantly, receive these phrases the way a young child receives loving words from a trusted caregiver: with openness, trust, and a willingness to be nourished.

These are the words your soul has been waiting to hear.

THE HEALING PHRASES:

Truth Phrases: For Physical Foundation & Security

1. Your body holds your truth and knows the way.

2. Your journey is perfect and unique to you.

3. Every breath brings a new beginning.

4. Your story is still being written.

5. You were never not whole.

6. Your body holds memories, yes, but it also holds freedom.

7. You were always worthy of tender care, of being touched with reverence, of being seen with eyes of wonder.

8. Your very existence is a miracle that needs no justification.

9. The child in you who longed to feel safe and secure is being held closely now.

10. You are safe. You are held. You are home.

11. Longings are not your weakness but a powerful call for your soul to return to the wholeness that you once knew.

Beauty Phrases: For Heart Connection & Emotional Healing

1. Your essence remains as beautiful as the day you were born.

2. Your presence is a gift to the world.

3. In your vulnerability lies your greatest strength.

4. You are safe to feel all your feelings fully.

5. Your heart knows the way to healing.

6. Dearest Heart, in this sacred pause, feel the gentle awakening of your soul's natural beauty.

7. Each emotion that flows through you is worthy of honour.

8. Your heart holds the beauty of a thousand sunsets, the wonder of every star, every flower, every meadow and seashore.

9. Your unique way of seeing the world, your creative spirit, your capacity for wonder—these were never meant to be dimmed.

10. You were always worthy of being delighted in, of having your inner world received with genuine interest.

11. Your love grows within you, so beauty grows. For love is the beauty of the soul.

12. You are a soul companion. We are all soul companions to each other.

Goodness Phrases: For Individual Purpose & Spiritual Growth

1. Your voice matters and deserves to be heard.

2. You are worthy of being seen and understood.

3. Your uniqueness is needed in this world.

4. You are held in unwavering faithfulness.

5. Your inner light never dims; it only gets clouded.

6. We are all expressions of God, of Divine Source, whatever name feels good to you: we are made of unconditional love.

7. Your inner guidance cannot be diminished by doubt or fear. It simply awaits your recognition.

8. Your spirit holds a purpose that only you can fulfill, a goodness that seeks expression through your unique gifts.

9. Your voice matters. Your thoughts are worthy of expression.

10. You are free to think, to create, to become.

11. This freedom is the essence of your spirit, now and always.

Connection Phrases: For Authentic Relationship

1. In every encounter lies the possibility of sacred connection.

2. Every meeting carries the potential for transformation.

3. In connection we find our way home.

4. Your presence brings healing to others.

5. I see the light in you that helps me see my own.

Wisdom Phrases: For Inner Knowing

1. What you desperately seek lives already within you.

2. In stillness, your wisdom speaks clearly.

3. You are both the seeker and the finder.

4. In the pauses between words lies deep wisdom.

5. You came with specific gifts waiting to be discovered.

Freedom Phrases: For Liberation

1. You are free to choose again in each moment.

2. There is space for all of who you are.

3. Your place is where eyes meet eyes with kindness.

4. You are here to dream infinitely.

5. Every experience opens the door to new learning.

These phrases carry the medicine of all three phases of childhood development:

- the security and grounding of the body (ages 0–7);

- the emotional connection and beauty of the heart (ages 7–14); and

- the individual purpose and spiritual awakening of the mind (ages 14–21).

FROM SPIRITUAL MOTHER ESSENCE

HEALING PHRASES

1. You are deeply loved, just as you are.
2. Your feelings are valid, and I am here to listen to whatever you want to say.
3. It's safe to express yourself and share your thoughts.
4. You are enough, and you always have been.
5. Every part of you is beautiful and worthy.
6. You are never alone; I am always with you.
7. It's okay to make mistakes; they are part of learning.
8. Your dreams and wishes matter to me.
9. You have the strength to overcome any challenge.
10. It's wonderful to be curious and ask questions.
11. Your creativity is a gift; let it shine.
12. You deserve joy and happiness in your life.
13. It's okay to rest and take care of yourself.
14. You are a unique soul with a special purpose.

15. Your laughter brings light and joy to the world.

16. It's important to play and have fun; life is a gift.

17. You are brave, and I admire your courage.

18. You are worthy of all the good things life has to offer.

19. You can trust your intuition; it will guide you.

20. Remember, you are loved unconditionally, always.

21. You are perfect just as you are in this moment.

22. Every feeling you have is a part of your journey.

23. It's okay to be different; your uniqueness is a strength.

24. You are deserving of love and kindness from yourself.

25. Your past does not define who you are today.

26. You are free to be your true self without fear.

27. It's okay to change and grow; that's part of life.

28. You are a precious being, worthy of respect and care.

29. You have the power to create your own happiness.

30. Your voice matters; speak your truth with confidence.

31. You are surrounded by love, always supporting you.

32. It's okay to let go of what no longer serves you.

33. You can embrace each moment with an open heart.

34. You are capable of deep compassion for yourself and others.

35. It's alright to feel vulnerable; it's a sign of strength.

36. You are deserving of forgiveness, both from yourself and others.

37. You are a beautiful expression of life's creativity.

38. You can trust that everything unfolds as it should.

39. You are a source of light in this world; shine bright.

40. Embrace all parts of yourself; you are whole and complete.

QUICK REFERENCE GUIDE: FINDING SUPPORT FOR YOUR JOURNEY

Note: While specific chapters are recommended for each challenge, healing is holistic. You may find valuable insights throughout the book. Trust your intuition about what sections call to you.

PHYSICAL & EMBODIMENT CHALLENGES

- Feeling disconnected from your body → Chapter 5: The Twelve Senses as Gateways
- Difficulty with physical boundaries → Chapter 8: The Architecture of Being
- Struggle with self-care → Chapter 7: Authentic Attachment
- Physical tension/anxiety → Chapter 5: The Twelve Senses as Gateways
- Sleep difficulties → Chapter 8: The Architecture of Being
- Eating/nourishment issues → Chapter 7: Authentic Attachment

EMOTIONAL & RELATIONSHIP CHALLENGES

- Difficulty expressing emotions → Chapter 9: The Heart Space Awakens
- Fear of intimacy → Chapter 7: Authentic Attachment
- Trust issues → Chapter 7: Authentic Attachment
- Relationship patterns repeating → Chapter 10: The Social Heart
- Feeling emotionally overwhelmed → Chapter 9: The Heart Space Awakens
- Difficulty with boundaries → Chapter 10: The Social Heart
- Parent-child connection struggles → Chapter 7: Authentic Attachment
- Sibling rivalry issues → Chapter 10: The Social Heart

MENTAL & IDENTITY CHALLENGES

- Negative self-talk → Chapter 11: The Awakening Mind and Spirit
- Perfectionism → Chapter 11: The Awakening Mind and Spirit
- Decision-making difficulty → Chapter 11: The Awakening Mind and Spirit
- Unclear sense of purpose → Chapter 11: The Awakening Mind and Spirit
- Fear of speaking up → Chapter 12: Sacred Listening Practice
- Imposter syndrome → Chapter 11: The Awakening Mind and Spirit

SPIRITUAL & CONNECTION CHALLENGES

- Feeling disconnected from Spirit → Chapter 6: Our Path to Birth
- Loss of wonder/joy → Chapter 3: Innocent Perception, A Place of Wonder
- Crisis of meaning → Homecoming: The Return to the Sanctuary
- Difficulty trusting life → Chapter 6: Our Path to Birth
- Feeling isolated → Chapter 2: The Journey for Connection
- Loss of creativity → Chapter 9: The Heart Space Awakens

PARENTING CHALLENGES

- Unsure about developmental stages → Chapter 4: Childhood Revisited and The Learning Journey
- Discipline difficulties → Chapter 7: Authentic Attachment
- Communication struggles → Chapter 12: Sacred Listening Practice
- Setting healthy boundaries → Chapter 10: The Social Heart
- Supporting emotional development → Chapter 9: The Heart Space Awakens
- Building secure attachment → Chapter 7: Authentic Attachment

PROFESSIONAL CHALLENGES (TEACHERS/CAREGIVERS)

- Creating nurturing environments → Chapter 8: The Architecture of Being
- Supporting diverse needs → Chapter 4: Childhood Revisited and The Learning Journey

- Building community → Chapter 10: The Social Heart

- Managing group dynamics → Chapter 10: The Social Heart

- Professional boundaries → Chapter 12: Sacred Listening Practice

- Self-care for caregivers → Chapter 7: Authentic Attachment

LIFE TRANSITION CHALLENGES

- Major life changes → Chapter 2: The Journey for Connection

- Identity shifts → Chapter 11: The Awakening Mind and Spirit

- Loss and grief → Chapter 9: The Heart Space Awakens

- New beginnings → Chapter 6: Our Path to Birth

- Career transitions → Chapter 11: The Awakening Mind and Spirit

- Relationship changes → Chapter 10: The Social Heart

PRACTICE & INTEGRATION SUPPORT

- Daily meditation practices → Homecoming: Return to the Sanctuary

- Body-based practices → Chapter 5: The Twelve Senses as Gateways

- Journaling prompts → Refer to the companion workbook

- Community building → Chapter 10: The Social Heart

- Creative expression → Chapter 9: The Heart Space Awakens

- Nature connection → Chapter 9: The Heart Space Awakens

FINDING YOUR WAY IN THE THREE-PHASE JOURNEY

- Early childhood challenges (ages 0–7) → Part One: Truth in the Body
- Middle childhood issues (ages 7–14) → Part Two: Beauty in the Soul
- Adolescent development (ages 14–21) → Part Three: Goodness in the Spirit
- Inner child healing → Chapters 6–8 and Healing meditations
- Reconnecting with feelings → Chapters 9–10 and Beauty meditations
- Finding your voice → Chapters 11–12 and Goodness meditations

WORKING TOGETHER:
AN INVITATION TO THE LISTENING
SANCTUARY

"Remember, the entrance to the sanctuary is inside you."
~ Rumi

O ver the last decade, I've mentored people into a deeper presence, helping them bring their authentic selves into their relationships and daily life. It is what I love to do more than anything else. I currently work with individuals and small groups, guiding them through the content of this book to transform their understanding of childhood, embrace all parts, and enhance their capacity for meaningful connection.

When we meet—whether one-to-one or in a small Listening Sanctuary—we'll focus on specific chapters that resonate with your current situation. What I've found over decades of practice is that something powerful happens when two or more people create space for authentic sharing: solutions appear that weren't visible before, and the wisdom that has always been waiting within you begins to surface.

For parents, we explore ways to support your child's development in everyday challenges. For teachers, we develop approaches to create classrooms where children feel truly seen. And for anyone seeking more meaningful connections, we practice the listening techniques from Chapter 12 that transform how we relate to others.

These sessions balance practical application with deeper understanding—helping you identify childhood patterns that might be influencing your present relationships while developing clear and gentle ways to address them. The result is a transformational shift in how you relate to yourself and others, bringing more ease, understanding, and joy to your daily interactions.

I bring to this work the patient, nurturing energy that awakened in me as a grandmother—a quality of deep, unhurried listening that creates space for your own wisdom to emerge. My approach is never to take away your power or to position myself as the expert in your life, but rather to walk beside you with the accumulated wisdom from working with families and teachers, and the profound truths I've discovered within my own family relationships and friendships. Together, we'll uncover the knowing that has always lived within you, waiting to be recognized.

How We Can Work Together:

- **One-to-One Journey**: Personalised sessions focussing on your specific questions, childhood patterns, and current challenges, with tailored support for your unique situation.

- **Small-Group Listening Sanctuaries**: Join a carefully curated circle where we practice deep listening together, supporting each other's growth and exploring messages from this book.

- **School and Community Workshops:** Tailored programmes for teachers, parents, and community groups designed to enhance relationships and create environments where everyone can thrive.

If you feel drawn to this work to enhance your parenting, teaching, or any relationship that matters deeply to you, I would be honoured to walk beside you on this path. To arrange a conversation about possibilities, find me by scanning the QR code below.

EMERGENCY RESOURCES

If you're experiencing acute crisis or need immediate support (UK):

- **Samaritans:** 116 123
- **Mental Health Emergency:** 0300 304 7000
- **Child Protection Services:** 0808 800 5000

This book is meant to support your journey but does not replace professional medical or mental health care when needed.

"The golden rules which must be embraced by the teacher's whole being, not held as theory, are: Reverent gratitude to the world in the person of the child which we contemplate every day, for the child presents a problem set us by divine worlds: Thankfulness to the universe. Love for what we have to do with the child. for the Freedom of the child—a freedom we must not endanger; for it is to this freedom we educate the child, that he may stand in freedom in the world at our side." (Source: V. How Knowledge Can Be Nurture - GA 305. Spiritual Ground of Education - Rudolf Steiner Archive)

ACKNOWLEDGEMENTS

In the journey of creating this book, I have been blessed by countless sacred encounters—with those souls who appeared at precisely the moment they were needed, each bringing a unique gift to this work.

I am profoundly grateful to my mentor, Sally Jenkinson, author of *The Genius of Play*, whose faith, positivity, and deep wisdom supported not only our school but my own understanding of childhood. Your dedication of time and love has rippled through countless lives.

To my tutor at Emerson College UK, the late Erika Grantham, who guided me through my training alongside Sally Jenkinson: your quiet strength and sharing of the gifts of Waldorf early years education continues to inspire all you touched.

To Renate Long-Breipohl, pioneer of Waldorf education in Australia, whose beautiful inspiring writing, deep insights and generous training support in Hong Kong also helped shape our school's reverent approach to childhood.

To my beloved colleagues and fellow "Witches of Westwick"—Amy Punton and Delia Sesiu—your wisdom, laughter, and shared cauldron of insights have been essential ingredients in this work. Our conversations continue to resonate through these pages.

To dear Lynne Kirk, whose love of storytelling illuminates how we shine when following our true calling, showing that purpose and passion light us from within.

To my long-term Hong Kong friends, Shona Smith and Cheryl Raper—there from the beginning—whose consistent showing up for connection over the years has become like solid ground beneath my feet: your loyalty and our shared experiences as parents and professionals have been a source of comfort through all the ups and downs.

To my friend Rowena Markies for your unwavering loyalty of friendship and the gift of your listening presence as you held space for my evolving thoughts.

To Sarah Rees for supporting me with your friendship and kindness and bringing inspiration through your love of neuroscience, your fascinating study of imitation, the wandering mind, and the developing imagination.

To Dr. Tessabella Lovemore for your beautiful courses on Active Practical Love that helped articulate and show how to practice what the heart already knows.

To Briar Grimley, my online friend and deeply connected listening partner, whose encouragement, support, and dedication have been a beautiful source of strength—proving that true connection transcends physical distance.

To my fellow authors from our Sedona author adventure—Taylor Victoria Nelson and Jenn Koch—for those days of deep, heartfelt connection. Though we had never met before, but called together for immediate purpose, we are now forever connected, supporting each other's creative journeys into the future.

To Keira Brinton, founder of JOA Publishing and the Mosai Network: thank you for your unwavering courage and inspiration. Your ability to ignite action and connect with authentic creative spirit added fuel to the fire.

To Juliet Wright who brought the book's heart to life, helping create a beautiful cover design, turning simple artwork into an invitation to something deeper.

To my editor, Mindy Peterman, for her compassionate and dedicated time for the final read-through. Together, we prayed and processed, ensuring that the essential message would be shared with depth, integrity, and purpose. Also, thank you to all the whole dedicated team at JOA publishing for your support.

To Grace Chow, for the beautiful illustrations of the doorways and the babies for chapters in the book! Grace shared her wonderful nurturing and creative gifts with Highgate House for many years, as she led loving and caring parent and child groups, her speciality being in supporting children under three.

To the incredible teachers and parents who have walked with me and those who still walk beside me: we discovered together; we learned to truly see children, to create spaces where every child's spirit can breathe and grow. We found that teaching and parenting is less about instruction and more about being present and connected. Together, we uncovered the magic of listening, of the abundance of creative, free, imaginative play, and of letting children unfold in their own beautiful way.

To all those whose paths have crossed mine—the authors whose books opened new worlds, and the ones whose words sparked inspiration and love—and all those I've yet to meet: "There are truly no strangers," as

Valarie Kaur beautifully reminds us, in her work, *Revolutionary Love*. We are all connected, intertwined, each encounter forming a strand in the whole tapestry of human experience.

Each of you is a sacred light along this path. My deepest gratitude to you for being exactly who you are, exactly when you were needed.

ABOUT THE AUTHOR

Julie Lam's journey began with a simple yet profound realization: the disconnection she witnessed in a Hong Kong nursery school wasn't inevitable—it was a call to create something better.

What started as a mother's protective instinct evolved into four decades of pioneering work in early childhood education. After founding Highgate House School in Hong Kong—a sanctuary where children and families experience the warm, gentle welcome every soul deserves— Julie has dedicated her life to understanding how we truly connect, both with the children in our care and the child that lives within us all.

Drawing from Steiner's anthroposophy, Pikler's respectful caregiving approach, and her own deep study of play therapy and meditation, Julie offers more than educational philosophy. Through her lived experience she reveals how childhood's three stages—Truth in the Body, Beauty in the Soul, and Goodness in the Spirit—hold the keys to healing our deepest disconnections.

Julie's work has touched thousands of families across continents, creating ripples of transformation that extend far beyond classroom walls. Alongside her ongoing educational work, she now nurtures what she calls "Listening Sanctuaries," serving as a gentle guide for those seeking to reconnect with their authentic selves and create meaningful relationships.

Her approach is never to position herself as the expert in your life but rather to walk beside you with the patient, nurturing energy that has always been her gift—but found its truest voice in her role of grandmother—helping you uncover the wisdom that has always lived within you, just waiting to be recognized.

From the Heart of Childhood emerges not as a manual of instructions but as a heartfelt offering drawn from lived experience, illuminating pathways back to the presence and connection we all seek.